Herbert Puchta & Jeff Stranks
G. Gerngross C. H[illegible] ...nes

American MORE! 4

Workbook

HELBLING LANGUAGES
CAMBRIDGE UNIVERSITY PRESS
editora ática

UNIT 1 Football? Soccer?

2 **1 Complete the dialogue using the words below. Then listen and check.**

been   bought   doing   for   lived   looking   see   since   visiting   wanted

Jess Hi, Emma!

Emma Hi! Sorry I'm late. Wow, what are all these people [1]........................ here today?

Jess The football stadium isn't far from here. There must be a game today. It's funny, I've [2]........................ here [3]........................ I was born, but I've never been to the stadium before. Have you ever been to a football game?

Emma Yes, I've [4]........................ to a few games—high-school games! Hey, do you [5]........................ that cute guy over there? I think he's lost … Hello! Are you [6]........................ for the stadium?

Zach Oh, hi. Yes, I am!

Jess It's not far from here. Just walk straight ahead and then turn right at the end of the street. Where are you from?

Zach I'm from Colorado. I'm just [7]........................ .

Emma How long have you been here?

Zach [8]........................ a week. I've always [9]........................ to see a professional football game … Have you [10]........................ tickets, too?

Jess No, we aren't going to the game. We're going to have lunch! Do you want to join us before the game starts? There's a good place to eat close to the stadium.

Zach OK! That sounds great!

2 Answer the questions.

1 Why does Emma say she's sorry?
2 Why are there so many people around?
3 How long has Jess lived in the area?
4 Where does Zach live?
5 Why is he in town?

Talking on the phone

3 **3 Listen to two dialogues. Match the speaker and the activity.**

1 Max	a) doing homework
2 Kelly	b) shopping
3 Eve	c) traveling somewhere

4 **4 Listen again and answer the questions.**

1 What is Kelly thinking of buying?
2 Who is Max meeting?
3 What is he doing this weekend?
4 Where is Eve?

Language Focus

Vocabulary Sports apparel

1 **List the items that each person is wearing. Then write the correct letter next to each sport.**

cleats glove goggles helmet pads
shirt shorts socks sneakers tank top

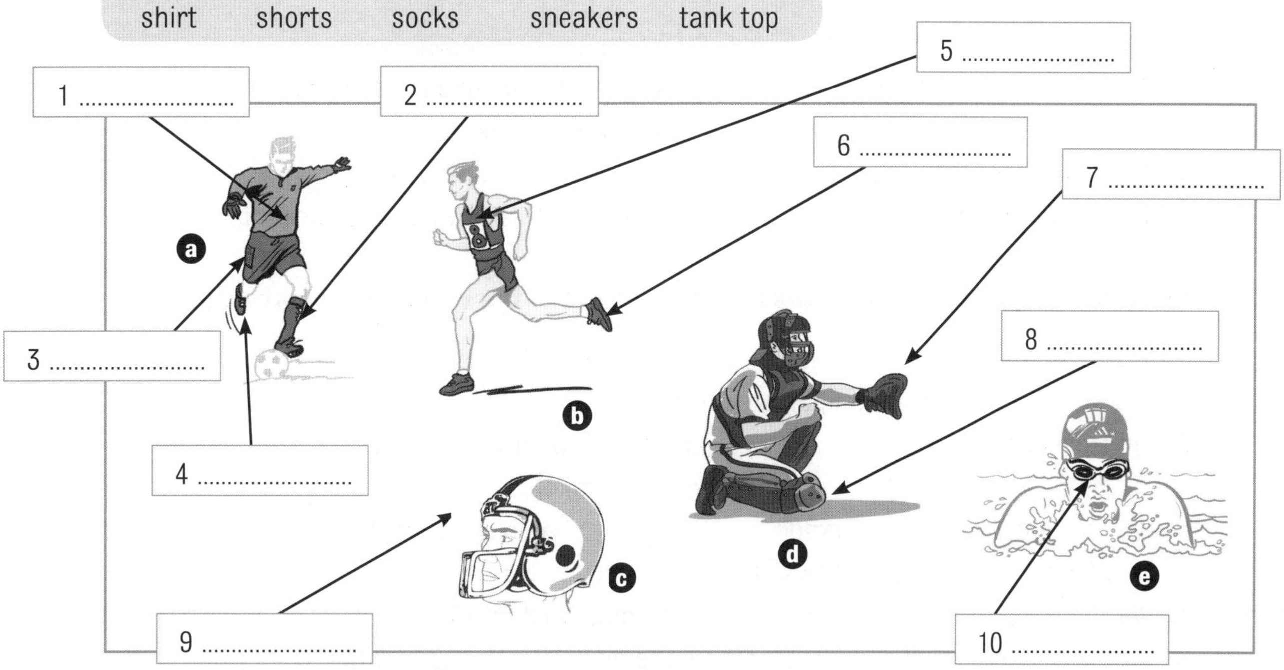

football .... swimming .... running .... soccer .... baseball ....

2 **Which words from Exercise 1 can be used with *a pair of* ...? Write them below.**

1 ....
2 ....
3 ....
4 ....
5 ....
6 ....
7 ....

Buying things in a sporting goods store

5 **3** **Complete the dialogue using the words below. Then listen and check.**

help pair size try

Salesclerk Can I [1]............................ you?
Customer Yes, I need a [2]............................ of bike shorts.
Salesclerk OK. What [3]............................ are you?
Customer About a 10, I think.
Salesclerk OK, why don't you [4]............................ these on?
Customer Thanks.

Grammar

Simple present / present continuous / present perfect (review)

1 **Write the number of the sentences in the correct place in the table.**

Habits, routines	Things happening now	Experiences someone has had up to now
2		

1 Have you ever been to Egypt?
~~2 What time do you get up?~~
3 What are you listening to?
4 Are you surfing the Internet?
5 Where do they play baseball?
6 What's the best movie you've ever seen?
7 What have you done to your hair?
8 Who are you talking to?
9 Are you scared of heights?
10 What are you studying in science this semester?

2 **Complete the sentences with the present perfect of the verbs in parentheses.**

1 What's that nice smell? .... fresh bread? (you make)
2 I .... to learn Spanish. (always want)
3 I'm sure I know you. .... somewhere before? (we meet)
4 .... your library books back? (you take)
5 I'm not ready to run a marathon. I .... enough. (not train)
6 How long .... the same hairdo? (you have)
7 We .... a test for about two months. (not have)
8 Maybe that letter will arrive later today. The mail .... (not come) yet.

3 **Circle the correct verb.**

1 **A** Sarah! Can you pick up the phone? It's someone for you.
B I can't come now. *I wash/I'm washing* my hair!
2 **A** Why aren't you eating your hamburger?
B It's disgusting. *I'm not liking/I don't like* it.
3 **A** Can I borrow your phone for a minute?
B Not right now. *I wait/I'm waiting* for an important call.
4 **A** Have you finished that book?
B No, *I still read/I'm still reading* it.
5 **A** Where's Alan?
B I don't know. *I'm not seeing/I haven't seen* him for a long time.
6 **A** You know this town really well, don't you?
B Of course! *I've lived/I lived* here since I was born!

4 Read the email and answer the questions.

Hi Kate

How are you doing with your studying? I've just been studying for math, and I'm working on history now. French isn't a problem for me since I practice a few words and grammar structures every day.

Talk to you later.

Jan

1 What has Jan already studied? ....
2 What does she practice every day? ....
3 What is she studying right now? ....

5 Complete the questions and short answers.

1 Have Mike and Jenny *arrived*? (arrive) No, they ....
2 .... you .... your homework? (do) Yes, I ....
3 .... he .... the new U2 CD? (buy) Yes, he ....
4 .... your parents .... on vacation? (go) No, they ....

6 Complete each sentence with the correct tense of the verb in parentheses.

1 Hurry up! You .... on the phone since 10 o'clock! (be)
2 I .... usually .... *Lost* on TV. (not watch)
But this series .... really good during the past few weeks. (be)
3 James .... to karate lessons twice a week. (go)
4 I can't find my purse anywhere. Are you sure you .... it? (not see)
5 .... you .... any good books right now? (read)
6 I .... often .... crossword puzzles. (not do)
7 Shh! I .... to a really interesting talk show. (listen)

7 Match the questions and answers.

1 Have you ever ridden on a motorcycle?
2 Do you ever go mountain biking?
3 How long have you had that watch?
4 Has your hair always been blonde?
5 Have you finished the crossword puzzle?
6 What's the most exciting thing you've ever done?
7 Have you ever eaten deer?

a) For about four years.
b) I went snowboarding last year.
c) No, but I've done most of it.
d) No, I haven't. I'm a vegetarian!
e) No, I don't.
f) Yes, I have.
g) Yes, since I was born.

Skills

Listening

1 Look at the photo and the advertisement for a TV documentary and guess the answers to the questions.

1 Where and what do free-climbers climb?
   a) cliffs along the coast
   b) buildings in cities
   c) rocks in the country

2 What do they use to climb?
   a) ropes
   b) ladders
   c) bare hands

3 Why is Alain Robert called the human spider?
   a) He wears a Spiderman costume when he climbs.
   b) He uses ropes that make him look like a spider.
   c) He climbs vertically just like a spider.

4 How many climbs has he done?
   a) 10
   b) More than 50
   c) 50

Pick of the week on TV tonight

Free-climbing with the HUMAN SPIDER

A fascinating look at the life and climbs of Alain Robert.

6 **2 Listen and check your answers.**

Reading

3 **Read the article and answer the questions.**

Would you enjoy clinging to the vertical wall on the outside of a 90-floor office block with hundreds of people watching you from the ground—and police waiting to arrest you when you reached the top of the building? Well, it's just a normal day in the life of Alain Robert, "the human spider."

Alain is a world-famous French "free urban climber." Free-climbers like Alain don't usually use any ropes, helmets, or other safety equipment. They climb using just their bare hands and climbing shoes. It's one of the most dangerous extreme sports in the world. And Alain doesn't climb for fame or money, although he has earned money through climbing some buildings for advertising. For example, in 2003 he climbed a building in London, England, wearing a Spiderman costume, to promote the movie.

He began climbing rock cliffs as a young boy. His first "free climb" was when he was around 12. He'd forgotten his keys and couldn't get into his home on the seventh floor of an apartment building. So instead of waiting for his parents to come home, he climbed up the outside of the building and got in through an open window. He says that from that moment on, he wanted to be a climber.

Since then, he has climbed more than 80 of the world's tallest buildings, often without permission. He has been arrested several times after these climbs, and has had five serious falls in his life. But none of these experiences has stopped him from attempting more and more dangerous climbs.

He admits that he puts his life in danger every time he climbs, but he says that climbing this way has now become "a habit." Which building is he planning to climb next? We'll have to wait and see!

1 How long has Alain Robert been free-climbing?
2 How many buildings has he climbed?
3 Has anyone ever paid him for climbing? When? Why?
4 Has he ever had serious accidents?
5 Why do the police often arrest him after his climbs?
6 Which building is he planning to climb next?

Writing for your Portfolio

4 **Read the questions in Exercises 1 and 3 again. Write an imaginary interview with Alain Robert using the information from the article.**

Paragraph 1: Explain who Alain Robert is and why he is famous.
Paragraph 2: Write your questions and his answers.
Paragraph 3: Say what you think about Alain Robert and free-climbing.

UNIT 2 Space and beyond

7 **1 Complete the dialogue using the words below. Then listen and check.**

bored excited happy hungry nervous sad

1 Kathy What's up with the big smile, Nick?
Nick I've had some good news! Remember that competition I entered? Well, I've won!
Kathy No wonder you look so [1]........................ Congratulations!

2 Kathy I'm [2]........................ . There's nobody around to do anything with.
Mom Why don't you call Laura?
Kathy I called her this morning, but she'd already gone out.

3 Nick Shall we go get something to eat before the game?
Luke No, I had dinner before I left. I'm not very [3]........................ .

4 Kathy Are you feeling [4]........................ about the history final, too?
Luke Yes. And what's worse, I couldn't study the last unit. I lost my notes.
Kathy Why didn't you ask me to lend you mine?
Luke I called you last night, but you were already in bed!

5 Nick What's wrong, Kathy? You look so [5]........................ .
Kathy It's my grandfather. He cut himself badly while he was working in his yard yesterday. By the time he got to the hospital, he'd already lost a lot of blood. He's still in the hospital now.
Nick Oh, I'm so sorry to hear that. I hope he gets better soon.

6 Luke You must be really [6]........................ about going to Japan.
Kathy Yes, I can't wait! I've never been before, but I've heard it's amazing.

2 Answer the questions.

1 What did Nick find out about the competition he'd entered? ....
2 Why couldn't Kathy speak to Laura on the phone? ....
3 Who had already eaten, Nick or Luke? ....
4 Why wasn't Luke able to borrow Kathy's notes? ....
5 What was Kathy's grandfather doing before he had the accident? ....
6 Why was Kathy looking forward to going to Japan? ....

Giving reasons

3 Match the questions and answers.

1 Why are you so bored?
2 You look happy! What's happened?
3 You're jumping up and down! Why are you so excited?
4 Why aren't you hungry?
5 Why are you nervous?
6 Why do you look so sad?

a) Because I failed my music exam.
b) I just heard some amazing news!
c) Because I have to give a presentation in front of the whole school, in English!
d) Because we're winning the game! Look at the score!
e) Because I finished my book and I have nothing to do.
f) Because I had so much to eat at lunchtime.

Language Focus

Vocabulary Travel

1 Match the pictures and captions. Then number the pictures in the correct order.

The plane takes off. ....
He gets to the airport. ....
Dave sets out on his trip. ....
The plane lands. ....

He gets on the plane. ....
He gets into the taxi. ....
He gets off the plane. ....
The flight takes four hours. ....

8 **2 Listen to the dialogue and answer the questions.**

1 What time did they set out? ....
2 What time did they get to the train station? ....
3 Why couldn't they get on the train right away? ....
4 How long did it take to get to Baltimore? ....
5 What time did they get off the train? ....

Talking about your trip to school

9 **3 Complete the dialogue. Use the prepositions below. Then listen and check.**

at off out on to (x 3) up

Tom How do you get [1]............................ school every day?
Claire I walk [2]............................ the bus stop, then I get [3]............................ the school bus.
Tom So what time do you set [4]............................ in the morning?
Claire I get [5]............................ around seven, and I get [6]............................ the bus stop at about a quarter past eight.
Tom Does the bus stop right outside school?
Claire Yes, I get [7]............................ the bus at the main entrance to my school.
Tom What time do you arrive [8]............................ school?
Claire By about quarter to nine.

Grammar

Past continuous vs. simple past

1 Write sentences. Use the simple past and past continuous tenses.

Example:

2:30 Tony / talk / on his phone
2:32 the battery / go dead

Tony was talking on his phone when the battery went dead.

1 10:00 Gabriella / walk down the street
10:10 she / trip

....

2 11:00 We / do an exercise
11:05 the bell / ring

....

3 11:30 My parents / watch / TV
11:40 they / hear / a knock at the door

....

4 7:30 My sister / brush / her teeth
7:32 her tooth / fall out

....

5 8:15 We / eat / dinner
8:17 the lights / go out

....

2 Circle the action that happened first in each sentence.

1 I'd only had my skateboard for a week before it broke.
2 They scored when they'd only been playing for 10 minutes.
3 When I arrived, you'd already left.
4 Jane didn't come to the movie theater. She'd seen the movie.
5 Lily was washing her hair when the phone rang downstairs.
6 Who were you talking to when I saw you yesterday?
7 We'd driven for half an hour when we realized we were lost.
8 I'd known Jerry for two years when he came to our school.

3 Read the sentences and answer the questions.

1 a) While I waited for the train, I wrote some emails.
b) While I waited for the train, I was writing some emails.
Which speaker finished the emails, a or b? ....

2 a) When we got there, Patrick was fixing dinner.
b) When we got there, Patrick fixed dinner.
Which speaker smelled food when she arrived, a or b? ....

3 a) The teacher was scolding me when I laughed out loud.
b) The teacher scolded me when I laughed out loud.
Which speaker got into trouble for laughing, a or b? ....

Past perfect

4 Complete the sentences with the past perfect form of the verbs in parentheses.

1 **A** Why was the teacher angry with Ivan?
B Because he .... his homework for the second time last week. (not do)
2 I was just getting on the bus when I realized I .... my ticket. (forget)
3 When I got home, the rain .... (stop)
4 Suddenly I remembered where I .... her before. (meet)
5 I was disappointed to learn that I .... the test. (not pass)
6 The river bed was completely dry. It .... for a long time. (not rain)

Narrative tenses (review)

5 Complete the story with the past continuous, simple past, or past perfect form of the verbs in parentheses.

Three-year-old throws away family's money

A three-year-old girl [1]............................ (throw) all the money a Chinese couple [2]............................ (save) for several months out of the window of their apartment while her parents [3]............................ (sleep). "When I woke up, my purse was on the bed. It was open, but all the money inside it [4]............................ (disappear)," said the mother.
"I immediately asked my daughter what [5]............................ (happen), but she said she [6]............................ (not know). I looked everywhere! When I saw a couple of bills on the windowsill, I realized what she [7]............................ (do)."
The owner of a restaurant below the apartment said he saw the money as it came flying down from the sky. "People in the street [8]............................ (go) crazy trying to catch it," he explained.
The couple said that they [9]............................ (hope) for a miracle to bring the money back.
Soon after the incident, the couple [10]............................ (cover) their windows with wire netting.

6 Read the story in Exercise 5 again. Find an example in 1–10 above of the following:

1 the simple past ....
2 the past continuous ....
3 the past perfect ....
4 an irregular past tense verb ....
5 a regular past tense verb ....

Skills

Reading

1 **Read the interview with Dr. Andrew Wilson, an astronaut. Write the interviewer's questions (a–e, below) in the correct spaces.**

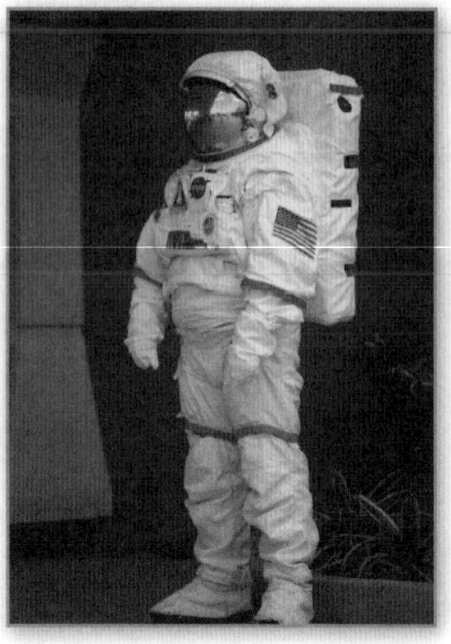

1 ....
It was while I was watching the launch of a space shuttle in 1981 on TV. I was studying at college at that time and I thought to myself, "I would like to be on a space shuttle one day." So I decided to do some research. I sent a letter to NASA, and they replied and told me how to go about following my dreams!

2 ....
The first flight I made was to get used to space and the International Space Station. But what I really wanted to do was take a longer flight and stay on the station for a few months.

3 ....
They've always been very supportive, ever since I was a young boy. I used to read books from the library about being an astronaut when I was just a kid! So I don't think they were too surprised when I made the decision to become an astronaut.

4 ....
I've thought about this a lot. In my work I'm often away from my wife and children for long periods of time. But a mission to Mars would mean a very long separation, probably several years. I might consider it when my children have grown up and gone to college. But right now they are young, and I don't want to be away from them for so long.

5 ....
The main thing you'd need to do is study to become an engineer, scientist, or doctor. Then, after you've had some experience, you need to look for ways of doing space research. And then … it's over to you! Being an astronaut is the most amazing experience anyone can ever have.

a) What advice would you give to teenagers interested in being astronauts?
b) What was the first flight you ever took?
c) Have you ever considered going to Mars?
d) When did you decide that you wanted to be an astronaut?
e) What did your parents think about your career choice?

2 **Circle T (True) or F (False) for the sentences below.**

1 Andrew was in college in 1981. T / F
2 NASA gave him useful information about becoming an astronaut. T / F
3 His parents were shocked at his decision to become an astronaut. T / F
4 He hasn't decided yet whether or not he wants to go to Mars. T / F
5 You need to go to college before you can become an astronaut. T / F

Listening

10 **3** **Listen. What event is each speaker talking about?**

a) The *Challenger* space disaster in 1986

b) The first landing on the moon in 1969

11 **4** **Listen again and say what each speaker was doing when they heard about the event.**

	Event	**What was he/she doing?**
Speaker 1	....	....
	....	....
Speaker 2	....	....
	....	....

Writing for your Portfolio

5 **Think about an important event that you heard about. What were you doing at the time? Write a paragraph describing what you were doing and how you felt when you heard the news.**

UNIT 3 Shopping

12 **1 The underlined words are in the wrong place in the dialogue. Write them in the correct place. Then listen and check.**

Katie I love what you're wearing, Nicola! Have you been on a shopping waste [1]..? Everything's new!

Nicola Well, yes, everything's new to me, but none of these clothes are really new, if you know what I mean.

Katie Really? You mean they're online [2].. clothes? I'd never buy anything someone else has worn.

Nicola Well, you really shouldn't [3].. try it. Buying used things is a great way to recycle and save money. That's why I think online auction sites are such an amazing thing. I mean, it's such a spree [4].. buying new things all the time when you could easily reuse something else.

Katie I prefer paying for things in debit card [5].. , though. At least people can't get information about your bank account if you just hand over cash.

Nicola Oh, I think it's safe to tell your cash [6].. number to websites that have good security. But I agree, you should [7].. give that information to just anyone. Especially not secondhand [8].. . It can be very dangerous.

2 Write *Katie* or *Nicola*. Who ...

1 often buys recycled clothing? ....
2 doesn't trust debit cards? ....
3 buys things online? ....
4 prefers to pay in cash? ....

Saying what people ought to do

3 Match the sentences and the advice.

1 I never seem to have enough money.
2 My hair keeps falling into my eyes.
3 My computer keeps crashing.
4 I have a headache.
5 I think someone is using my bank account.

a) You should get someone to fix it.
b) You shouldn't read right now.
c) You should tell your bank immediately.
d) You should save more.
e) You should get it cut.

Language Focus

Vocabulary Money and shopping

1 Find words about shopping. Look up and down. Write the words next to their definitions.

1 bills or coins that you pay with

_ _ _ _

2 a special paper that you sign and pay with

_ _ _ _ _

3 shopping that you do on the Internet

_ _ _ _ _ _

4 things that aren't new are

_ _ _ _ _ _ hand

S C A S T R B E
A A S O S R E N
L S S P E D A S
C H E C K E N P
R O C C O B E R
E X O N L I N E
D E N O N T T E
I N D E B T E D
T I L L R I R E

2 Match the pictures with the captions.

a 

b 

c 

d 

e 

1 Can I pay by debit card? ....
2 It's very expensive. We can only afford to window shop here! ....
3 It's secondhand, but it looks brand new! ....
4 Sorry, we only take cash or cards, no checks. ....
5 Look at her! She's been on a shopping spree! ....

Talking about shopping

13 **3 Complete the dialogues with words and phrases from Exercises 1 and 2. Then listen and check.**

1 **Customer** These fit me really well. I'll take them. Can I pay by [1]........................?
Salesclerk Sorry, it's [2]........................ only. No checks or cards.

2 **Will** What an amazing jacket!
Amy I know. It's a genuine 1950s one. I found it in a [3]........................ store.

3 **Caitlin** I hope you're not taking me on a [4]........................ . I don't have any money.
Carrie Neither do I, but we can always [5]........................ .

Grammar

Should(n't) / ought

1 **Match the problems and the advice.**

1 I keep losing my keys!
2 I can't see the board in class.
3 I get an earache after listening to my MP3 player.
4 I feel bad about being so rude to Mandy.

a) You should apologize.
b) You should keep them in a safe place.
c) You shouldn't play it so loud.
d) You ought to have your eyes tested.

2 **Complete the sentences with *should, shouldn't*, or *ought*.**

1 **A** I have a toothache.
B You .... eat so much candy.
2 **A** I bought these pants a week ago and the zipper is already broken!
B You .... to take them back to the store.
3 **A** I'd really like to see *The Golden Compass*.
B I think you .... read the book first.
4 **A** My parents don't want me to go to the concert.
B I really don't think you .... to go.
5 **A** I have a temperature and a bad cough.
B Maybe you .... go to school today.

3 **Rewrite the second sentence so that it has the same meaning as the first. Use the words in parentheses.**

1 It's a good idea to get to the show early. (should)
We .... early.
2 It isn't a good idea to eat candy. (shouldn't)
You .... candy.
3 Watching movies in English can help you improve. (ought to)
You .... movies in English to improve.
4 It's rude to interrupt people when they're talking. (shouldn't)
You .... people when they're talking.
5 The best thing to do is ask the teacher to help you. (should)
You .... the teacher to help you.
6 A doctor is the person to see when you are sick. (ought to)
You .... when you are sick.

Gerunds

4 **Complete the description using the words below.**

being   cleaning   coming   performing   playing   teaching

Cleaner becomes professional guitarist

[1]............................ a song on a classical guitar one day has led to an Hispanic cleaner's new career as a guitar teacher.
A webcam filmed the man, who had a job [2]............................ offices and floors at a state university.
The president of the university then invited him to play at events around the campus.

Since then, his achievements have included [3]............................ on stage and [4]............................ classical guitar to students.
The man said that he became a cleaner after [5]............................ to the U.S., although [6]............................ a classical guitarist was always his lifelong dream.

5 **Complete the sentences with the gerund form of the verbs in parentheses.**

1 I have to clean the house on the weekends. .... the garbage out is the worst job! (take)
2 Michael loves .... He wants to go to drama school one day. (act)
3 .... for clothes is Jessie's favorite activity. (shop)
4 I don't think .... money on expensive designer clothes is worth it. (spend)
5 I hate .... My cakes are always a disaster! (bake)
6 It can be hard to get used to .... in a city. (drive)

6 **Read Holly's answers. Then complete the sentences.**

Do you .... ?	
play a musical instrument	Yes, I play piano. I practice every day.
listen to music	Yes, all the time. I love it.
jog in the park	No, I hate it.
clean the house	Yes, I clean my room every day.
shop for clothes	Yes, I love it!

Holly's regular activities include [1]................................ the piano, [2]................................ to music, [3]............................ her room, and [4]................................ for clothes. She doesn't like [5]................................ in the park.

Skills

Listening

14 **1** **Complete the dialogue using the words below. Then listen and check.**

debit card | window-shopping | cash | check | online

Sarah What are you looking for on the Internet?

Connor I'm looking for a copy of an old book I used to have as a child. But it looks like it's out of print now. None of the bookstores have it.

Sarah You should try an online auction site. I bet you'll find several copies of it there.

Connor I've never bought anything [1].............................. before.

Sarah You should try it! You can find some amazing things!

Connor How do you pay for things? You can't pay in [2].............................., can you?

Sarah Well, you usually have to give your [3].............................. number to make an online payment. But some sellers don't mind if you write them a [4].............................. . And, if you find someone who lives near you, you could even go and pick up the item and buy it with cash.

Connor Don't you have to be over 18 to register, though?

Sarah Yes. If you're younger than that, you should ask your parents to shop with you. Anyone can browse though! Come on, let's do some [5].............................. online in the meantime!

Reading

2 **Read the article and then match the sentence halves.**

A Life for Sale

John Freyer, a student at the University of Iowa, decided to sell everything he owned on the Internet. He and his friends tagged all his possessions and put them up for sale on an auction website to be sold to the highest bidder. "I invited about 50 people to my house for an 'inventory party,'" said Freyer. The items included an unopened box of taco shells, half a bottle of mouthwash, his clothes, and even unopened presents for his family.

Before long, Freyer's possessions found new homes all over the world. A chair ended up in the Museum of Modern Art. A bag of pork skins went to Japan. Then Freyer had another idea. He decided to track down and then visit his old possessions in their new homes.

After that, he wrote a book about his project. It is called *All My Life for Sale*. It tells the story of Freyer's life, his travels, and his thoughts about the objects in our lives.

He still keeps track of his old things and where they have ended up. On the website allmylifeforsale.com you can see where many of Freyer's belongings ended up. But of course, he doesn't own that website. It was his last possession to be sold.

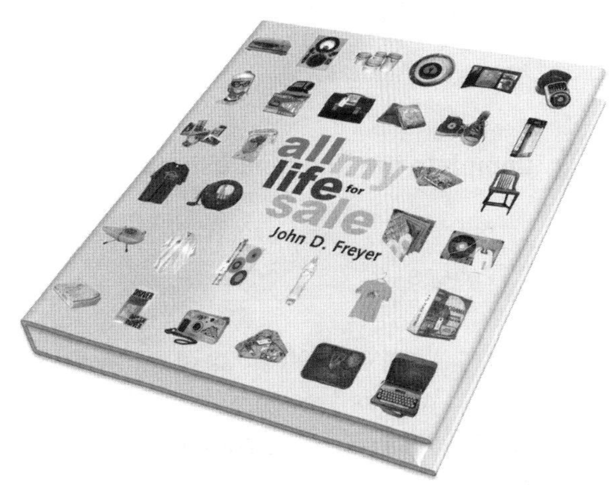

1 John Freyer
2 He sold
3 His clothes, everyday objects, and presents
4 After he sold his things, he
5 The last thing he sold
6 He is keeping track

a) went to visit them.
b) of what happened to his belongings after he sold them.
c) was his website.
d) everything he had online.
e) decided to sell everything he owned.
f) were included in the sale.

3 Find words in the article that mean ...

1 belongings ....
2 a sale to someone who pays the highest price ....
3 put price tags on ....
4 a list of property ....
5 someone who takes part in a sale where something is sold for the highest price ....
6 discover ....

Writing for your Portfolio

4 Imagine you are selling all your belongings online. Write a web page describing your life.

Paragraph 1: Give some background information about yourself.
Paragraph 2: Briefly describe your home, your town, and your free-time activities under three separate headings.
Paragraph 3: Say why you think your life would be a good thing for someone to buy!

UNIT 4 A working life

15 **1** **Complete the dialogue using the words below. Then listen and check.**

before	creative	going	hardworking	honest
college	soon as	taking	when	working with

Jon What are you going to do [1]........................ we graduate?
Beth Well, as [2]........................ we finish, I'm [3]........................ a vacation.
Jon Where are you going?
Beth I'm [4]........................ to Chile. I think it's important to see another country [5]........................ I go to college.
Jon Where will you go to [6]........................ ?
Beth I'm going to our state college to study to be a vet!
Jon You'd make a good vet. You are kind and patient. I think that's important when you're [7]........................ people or animals. I couldn't do a job like that. I wonder what my ideal job would be.
Beth You should think about working in advertising or something, since you're so [8]........................ .
Jon But I'm not sure I'm [9]........................ enough. I'm pretty lazy.
Beth Well, at least you're [10]........................ !

2 **Match these people and their ideal jobs.**

1 Nikita would be a good nurse
2 Paul should be a writer
3 Marek would be good at sales
4 Jessica should go into business
5 I think Isabel could easily work on her own
6 Ben could be a company president in a few years

a) because she's responsible and efficient.
b) because she likes helping people.
c) because she's very independent.
d) because he's hardworking and very ambitious.
e) because he's good at persuading people.
f) because he's imaginative and creative.

Saying what you want to do

16 **3** **Number the lines in the correct order. Then listen and check.**

Rosie .... I could never be a doctor.
Rosie .... I hate blood! Don't you?
Rosie .... I'm not sure yet, but I'm thinking of becoming an architect.
Rosie .... Well, I like design, and I'm good at math, too.
Sean .... Is there any job you'd never want to do?
Sean .... No, I don't mind it. I could be a doctor, I guess …
Sean .... What do you think you'd like about that?
Sean ....1..... What job do you want to do one day?
Sean .... Why not?

Language Focus

Vocabulary Personality adjectives

1 **Read the notes interviewers have made about a group of college applicants. Answer the questions.**

Student
A – calm, never in a rush
B – determined to get to the top quickly
C – wants to help whenever possible
D – very direct, doesn't say things that aren't true
E – will work very hard
F – relaxed, casual, not bossy

Which student is ... ?

1 easygoing ....
2 helpful ....
3 patient ....
4 hardworking ....
5 ambitious ....
6 honest ....

2 **Write the opposites of these adjectives in the correct column.**

ambitious	creative	efficient	friendly	helpful
honest	imaginative	kind	patient	polite

un	*im*	*dis*	*in*

Talking about personalities and jobs

3 **Complete the sentences with the opposites of the underlined adjectives.**

1 I could never be a waiter. I'm too <u>rude</u> and <u>unfriendly</u>!
To be a waiter, you have to be .... and ....
2 I could never be a farmer and get up early for work. I'm too <u>lazy</u>.
You have to be .... to be a farmer.
3 It's hard to imagine Ellen being a coach. She's so <u>impatient</u>.
You have to be .... to be a good coach.
4 I can't believe Annie's going to be a teacher. She's so <u>unkind</u> to children!
Teachers should be .... to children.
5 He shouldn't be a police officer. He's <u>not truthful</u> all the time.
Police officers need to be .... people.

Grammar

Talking about the future
be going to present continuous (review)

1 **Complete the sentences. Use *be going to* or the present continuous.**

1 I hate my hair. I .... it cut. (get)

2 I've just called the salon. Wish me luck! I .... it cut tomorrow afternoon. (have)

3 John's .... a speech at his sister's wedding next month. (give)

4 He .... an expensive suit. (rent)

5 I .... to New York tomorrow. (fly) It's .... 12 hours! (take)

6 I .... an exam this afternoon. (take) I know I .... well. (do)

2 **Which sentences ...**

1 ... are about someone's intentions? ....
2 ... are about fixed arrangements in the future? ....

3 **Complete the dialogue with *be going to* or the present continuous of the verbs in parentheses.**

Sarah I really like Mark. I want to get to know him better.
Jade So what are you going to do?
Sarah Well, I have an idea. I [1]................................. (invite) him to the concert.
Jade What concert?
Sarah Don't you know? I sing in a band, and we [2]................................. (play) at the dance tomorrow night. Why don't you come too?
Jade I can't. Tomorrow we [3]................................. (rehearse) for the school play.
Sarah What time does it finish? You could join us later. We [4]................................. (go) to a restaurant after the concert. It's [5]................................. (be) a lot of fun!
Jade Who [6]................................. (go)?
Sarah Just the band—and Mark—I hope!

Future time clauses

4 Circle the correct option.

1 *As soon as/Before you* travel to the U.S., you need to get a passport.
2 I always have a snack *after/before* getting home from school.
3 What are you doing *before/when* school finishes today?
4 *As soon as/ When* it rains, we have P.E. inside.
5 I'm going to get my driver's license *as soon as/after* I can.

5 Complete the second sentence so that it has a similar meaning to the first sentence. Use one of the words or phrases in the box below.

after	as soon as	before	when

1 *The exact moment* I get home, I'll call you.
I'll call you .... I get home.
2 I'll definitely visit the Taj Mahal *at the time* I go to India.
.... I go to India, I'll definitely visit the Taj Mahal.
3 Are you going to study again *at an earlier time than* your final exams?
Are you going to study again .... your final exams?
4 What are we going to do *when* the finals *are finished*?
What are we going to do .... finals?

6 Complete the sentences with the correct form of the verbs in parentheses.

1 I .... you a postcard when I .... to Florida. (send, get)
2 Promise me you .... me as soon as you .... the news. (call, hear)
3 What .... after you .... school? (you do, finish)
4 .... your dinner before you .... out, please. (finish, go)
5 If you .... your tickets online, it .... as expensive. (book, not be)
6 When you .... Carl again, ... him I said "hello". (see, tell)

7 Write five sentences using the future time clauses from Exercise 4.

1 ....
2 ....
3 ....
4 ....
5 ....

Skills

Listening

17 ① **Listen to the radio show about people's summer jobs. Write the number of the speaker next to the correct photo.**

a) testing movie DVDs

b) testing computer games

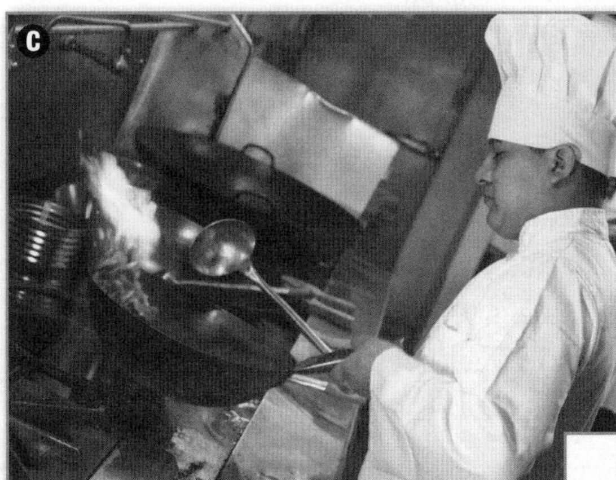

c) testing recipes

d) playing historical characters

e) making cotton candy at a zoo

Reading

2 **Read the article and answer the questions.**

You need to have a head for heights

Being fired doesn't bother Áron Molnar. In fact, it's part of his daily job.
That's because Áron is a human cannonball. Twice a day in the busy season, he flies out of a mouth of a cannon and through the air into a safety net at the other side of the circus ring.
Áron has always been close to the circus. His Hungarian parents met while they were both part of a circus, so becoming a circus performer was a natural choice of career for Áron. He started as an acrobat and trapeze artist, but he always wanted to be the human cannonball. As soon as there was a vacancy, he applied for the job.
It isn't an easy job, though. "There's more to my job than just climbing into the cannon and waiting for the burst of air that will send me flying," he says. "I have to fly straight, keep my body completely still, and then do a somersault in midair, so that I can land on my back in the net. All this has to be done in just two seconds!"

This is not a job for people who want to earn a lot of money. Yes, the actual working hours are much shorter than a normal nine-to-five job, but you have to live and move around with the circus, and although your act may last for only a few minutes, you have to be involved in the whole show, at every performance. You have to be physically strong, too. Áron spends several hours every day working on exercises to strengthen his knees and back. Every flight is a risk. One wrong move and there could be a very serious accident.
Is it worth the risk? Áron says, "Every time I work, I feel free, it's as if I'm flying. How many people can say that about their job?"

1 Why was Áron's career choice not unexpected? ....
2 Why would gymnastics training be useful in this job? ....
3 Why does he have to be strong? ....
4 Why is Áron's job risky? ....
5 What does Áron say he feels every time he works? ....

Writing for your Portfolio

3 **Read the advertisement. Write a letter saying why you want this job and what qualities and experience you have that make you suitable.**

Students! Are you looking for summer work?

Are you:

helpful, patient, kind, and friendly?
efficient and responsible?
hardworking?
creative and imaginative?

Club U.S. is looking for students aged 16-18 to work in a number of areas such as catering, working with pets and children, and working in arts at its international summer camps for children from the ages of 5 to 10.

UNIT 5 Bookworms

18 **1 Complete the dialogue using the words below. Then listen and check.**

boring	find out	get into	great	hang out
no way	put it down	so	such	turn into

Joe You want to do something tonight? We could play tennis or just [1]......................... at the gym.

Lucy Sorry, I'd rather stay in and read my book.

Joe That sounds so [2] .... ! You're always reading these days. You're going to [3] .... a real bookworm!

Lucy But it's such a [4] .... book. It's *Point Blanc*, the second Alex Rider book. Really, it's [5]......................... exciting, I just can't [6]......................... !

Joe What's it about?

Lucy Alex Rider has to pretend he's someone else, a boy named Alex Friend. His mission is to go to Point Blanc, a school for spoiled rich kids, in order to [7]......................... what's really going on there. He learns that it's a very strange place, with a lot of strange things happening … It's just [8]......................... a good book that I just don't want it to end.

Joe I enjoyed the first Alex Rider book. Even though it took me a while to [9]......................... , it was really good. This one sounds even better. Can I take a look at it?

Lucy [10]......................... , I'm still reading it!

2 Answer the questions.

1 What does Joe want to do?

....

2 Why doesn't Lucy want to stop reading?

....

3 What does Joe think of her plans to read instead of going to the gym?

....

4 What does Alex Rider discover at Point Blanc?

....

5 What did Joe think of the first Alex Rider book?

....

6 Why doesn't Lucy hand over the book to Joe?

....

Language Focus

Vocabulary Kinds of books

1 Match the book reviews 1–6 with the kinds of books a–f.

1 As usual, the sharp-eyed Private Investigator finds out that everyone has a motive for the murder. She uncovers all sorts of secrets in everyone's lives ....

2 This informative book tells us all about the life of Martin Luther King, Jr., from his birth in January 1929 in Atlanta, Georgia, in the South of the U.S. ....

3 O mother, mother, make my bed,
O make it soft and narrow:
My love has died for me today,
I'll die for him tomorrow.

4 The first few explore the themes of childhood and growing up seen through the eyes of a child. Finally, in the last one, "Behind the Bike Racks," the narrator is a teenager in high school.

5 Chapter 11: *Trouble shooting*
Make sure your digital camera is connected to the computer via the special USB provided. If this is not done, you will not be able to see the icon on the screen ....

6 Sadly, Lucinda stood on the bridge, looking down at the water as it flowed past her. And suddenly, he was there. Their eyes met across the reflections in the river. Lucinda knew he was the one she would marry.

a) biography ....
b) detective novel ....
c) nonfiction ....
d) poetry ....
e) romance ....
f) short story collection ....

Talking about books

19 **2 Complete the dialogue using the words below. Then listen and check.**

alright	detective	do you like	exciting
favorite	find out	like	love

Cameron 1.. comic books?
Evie Do you mean *Batman*, or something like that?
Cameron Yes. It's my 2.. kind of book.
Evie Hmm, they're 3.. , but I'm not crazy about them.
Cameron So what do you 4.. ?
Evie I like books that are 5.. , where you just can't wait to 6.. what happens in the end.
Cameron Do you like 7.. novels and crime stories?
Evie Yes, I 8.. that kind of book.

Grammar

So / such

1 Match the sentence halves.

1 Mrs. Green was so angry about the test scores
2 She drove so fast
3 The test was so difficult
4 She was so hungry
5 It was such an emotional play
6 She was such a good author

a) that she skidded and crashed.
b) that I couldn't answer any questions.
c) that she ate all her food in about two minutes.
d) that she gave us all extra homework.
e) that everyone wanted to read her books.
f) that everyone felt exhausted by the time it was over.

2 Circle the correct word.

1 It was *so/such* cold weather that they decided to close the school for the day.
2 The trip was *so/such* long that I wanted to sleep most of the way.
3 They gave me *so/such* a bad haircut that I won't ever go back there again.
4 I have *so/such* a lot of homework that I won't be able to go to bed before midnight.
5 The book was *so/such* boring that I didn't even finish it.
6 The movie was *so/such* sad that I spent most of the time in tears.

3 Add *so...that* or *such...that* and write sentences about the pictures.

1 He is / in love / he / walk / into a streetlight.

....

....

2 She / ate / fast / she / has / a stomachache.

....

....

3 It is / a big package / it / not fit / in the mailbox.

....

....

Phrasal verbs

4 Write the correct meaning of the verb + preposition at the end of each sentence.

1 Can you <u>turn up</u> the volume please? I can't hear it. ....
2 I wonder how many people will <u>turn up</u> at the event? ....
3 I wasn't looking and I <u>ran into</u> a tree!. ....
4 I <u>ran into</u> an old friend yesterday. ....
5 As soon as you <u>get into</u> the taxi, tell the driver where you want to go. ....
6 It's difficult to start a new book, but you'll soon <u>get into</u> it. ....

enter
attend
become used to
met by accident
increase
hit

5 Complete the sentences with the correct form of the phrasal verbs below.

take care of | look into | play around | run after

1 The police .... the robber, but they couldn't catch him.
2 "Stop .... , class, and finish your work!" said the teacher.
3 I'm not sure whether it will be possible to get tickets, but I'll .... it this afternoon.
4 You can borrow my MP3 player, but please .... it.

6 Circle the correct word.

1 It's a good idea to check *over/around* your work again before you turn it in.
2 I have to have a tooth taken *off/out*.
3 She's finding it hard to get *up/over* her grandmother's death.
4 There's so much to learn, I'm not sure I can take it all *up/in*.
5 What's the best way to put *away/out* a fire?
6 The surgeon is carrying *on/out* an operation this afternoon.

7 Replace the underlined expressions with the phrasal verbs below.

break up | find out | get over | put up | take after

1 Who do you <u>resemble</u> most in your family? ....
2 I'm trying to <u>get information</u> about tickets for the next game. ....
3 I'm sorry to hear you have a cold. I hope you <u>recover from</u> it soon. ....
4 To get more publicity for our show, we should <u>display</u> posters around the school. ....
5 I don't want to <u>end our relationship</u> because of what happened. ....

Skills

Reading

1 **Read these book reviews on a website. How many people didn't like the book?**

The End is the 13th and last book in *A Series of Unfortunate Events*, a set of books written by Lemony Snicket. It tells the story of the Baudelaire orphans. This is a great book. It's probably my favorite book ever. My only complaint is that this is the last one!
Gina

I thought the book was written in a rushed sort of way. It jumped around so much that it was sometimes difficult to know what exactly was going on. The details weren't all that good, but I still enjoyed it, although it's not the superstar book that everyone said it was. This book talks about other books in the series too much. And the story was very odd. I found it impossible to read!
Ronin

I took this book out from the library, thinking from the plot and the title that it would be good. But the story is very jerky, it skips around a lot, and at the end of the book, I wasn't sure what it was all about. A lot of the things the orphans did were far from believable. This book is OK, but not the greatest book I've ever read.
Tyler

This book is my favorite book. I couldn't stop reading it. The ending was moving. The book answered a lot of questions for me, but also left some questions unanswered. It was AMAZING!
Sophie

This book looked like it would be exciting, but it wasn't. I was very disappointed, because after only four chapters, I was already so bored with it that I didn't care what happened to any of the characters. I kept thinking it would get better, but I was wrong.
Abbie

At first it didn't really interest me. Then I started getting into it more. And I couldn't stop! I read it in around two days: now I wish I had taken more time to read it because I just didn't want it to end. It's the best book I've ever read. It was heartbreaking to finish it. I wish there was a sequel to this book.
Amina

2 **Read the reviews again and write the name of ...**

1 two readers who complain there isn't a sequel. ....
2 two readers who found the book confusing to follow. ....
3 two readers who rate the book as the best they've ever read. ....
4 one reader who thought the story wasn't very unusual. ....
5 two readers who thought the story was unusual. ....
6 two readers who couldn't put the book down. ....

3 **Write the underlined words from the reviews next to the correct meaning:**

1 a book that continues the story of an earlier book ....
2 emotional, leading to intense feelings ....
3 strange, not ordinary ....
4 unconnected ....
5 very sad ....

Listening

20 **4** **Listen to the conversation and check (✓) the answers for Luke and Ashley.**

What do you think about reading? (Check one box for each statement.)

	Strongly agree	Agree	Disagree	Strongly disagree
1 Reading is more for girls than boys.	Luke ☐ Ashley ☐	Luke ☐ Ashley ☐	Luke ☐ Ashley ☐	Luke ☐ Ashley ☐
2 Reading is boring.	Luke ☐ Ashley ☐	Luke ☐ Ashley ☐	Luke ☐ Ashley ☐	Luke ☐ Ashley ☐
3 Reading is important.	Luke ☐ Ashley ☐	Luke ☐ Ashley ☐	Luke ☐ Ashley ☐	Luke ☐ Ashley ☐
4 I can't find books that interest me.	Luke ☐ Ashley ☐	Luke ☐ Ashley ☐	Luke ☐ Ashley ☐	Luke ☐ Ashley ☐
5 I would be happy if someone gave me a book as a present.	Luke ☐ Ashley ☐	Luke ☐ Ashley ☐	Luke ☐ Ashley ☐	Luke ☐ Ashley ☐

Writing for your Portfolio

5 **Complete the questionnaire yourself. Then use it to write a paragraph about your reading habits. Explain why you agree or disagree with each statement.**

UNIT 6 The main event

21 **1 Complete the dialogue using the words and phrases below. Then listen and check.**

move	are you allowed	aren't allowed to	forbidden
let	goes off	shouldn't	return

Kiah Martin tells me you're going to a 3D show at the iMax theater next week. It's really cool! You'll love it. I went last month.

Oscar Oh, good, then I can ask you about it. [1]........................ to take pictures during the show?

Kiah No, they don't [2]........................ you use any cameras at all. Cameras are [4]........................ in the auditorium by law.

Oscar What about food? Are there any rules about that?

Kiah Well, you [4]........................ eat in the auditorium. But you can buy refreshments just outside, once the show is over. The other thing to remember is that you have to [5]........................ your glasses. If you don't return them, an alarm [6]........................! You also [7]........................ talk too loud. Oh, and some people think the seats [8]........................ during a show, but they don't.

Oscar Right! I'll remember all that.

22 **2 Listen again. Which of the following are allowed? Write A (allowed) or NA (not allowed).**

1 using a video camera ....
2 taking pictures ....
3 eating candy in the auditorium ....
4 wearing 3D glasses ....
5 talk softly ....
6 talk softly ....
7 drinking soda while you watch the movie ....
8 eating popcorn afterward ....

Talking about permission

3 Look at the rules. Then complete the answers to the questions. Use *allowed to*.

1 Why don't you take your cell phone?
We .... cell phones.
2 Why don't you wear earrings to school?
We .... to school.
3 Why don't you take your dog to school?
Dogs .... at school.
4 Why can't you take this book out of the library?
You .... home.
5 Why don't you ever wear your baseball cap to school?
We .... hats in school.

No hats allowed in school.

No jewelry in school.

No cell phones.

No pets.

These books can only be used in the library.

Language Focus

Vocabulary Special events

1 Circle the correct word to make phrases which describe special events.

1 a book *fair/tournament*
2 a car *show/museum*
3 a bike *fair/race*
4 a fashion *race/show*
5 a movie *exhibition/premiere*
6 a music *festival/night*
7 a school *fair/night*
8 a tennis *tournament/festival*

2 Write the number of the correct event from Exercise 1 in each photo.

Talking about events

23 **3 Number the lines in the correct order. Then listen and check.**

A .... Yeah, I love them, too. What about a fashion show? Have you ever been to one?
A .....*1*..... Have you ever been to a music festival?
A .... What were they like?
A .... What was it like?
B .... Really interesting. I think modeling must be hard work though.
B .... Yes, I went to Bonnaroo last year. I saw the Raconteurs play.
B .... Amazing. They're my favorite band.
B .... Yeah, my cousin's a model, so she got me a ticket once.

Grammar

The passive

1 Complete the sentences using the words below.

(not) allow attend hold play spend wear

1 Every year, a lot of money .... on music festivals around the world.
2 In a tennis tournament, a game of doubles .... by four players.
3 The latest fashions .... by models at a fashion show.
4 The World Series .... every year in North America.
5 The premiere of the movie .... by movie stars and celebrities.
6 Children .... in the pool without an adult.

2 Complete the opening lines of these newspaper articles with the past passive.

1 **Police arrest robber**

A robber .... by police last night...

2 **Air ambulance flies pop star to hospital**

A pop star .... to the hospital yesterday...

3 **Retired man wins race**

Yesterday, the annual 20km fun run ....by a man aged 72.

4 **Oscar Award for Hilary Swank**

Hilary Swank .... the Oscar for Best Actress at last night's LA ceremony.

5 **City elects new mayor**

The new mayor for the city .... last night...

6 **Millions watch the Super Bowl**

The Super Bowl .... by millions of people around the world on Saturday.

3 Complete the description with the present passive or past passive form of the verbs in parentheses.

Early tennis balls [1].......................... (make) in Scotland from sheep stomachs. These tennis balls [2].......................... usually [3].......................... (stuff) with wool from the animal. In the 18th century, strips of wool [4].......................... (wrap) tightly around into a little ball. Then string [5].......................... (tie) around the ball and the whole ball [6].......................... (cover) with a white cloth. Modern tennis balls [7].......................... (make) from rubber. They [8].......................... then [9].......................... (cover) with a soft material called felt.

Make / let / be allowed to

4 **Complete the sentences with the correct form of *make, let,* or *allow.***

1 Are you .... to go out late at night?
2 What time do your parents .... you come home?
3 Do your parents .... you to play computer games in your bedroom?
4 Will you .... me borrow your laptop this weekend?
5 We aren't .... to wear jewelry to school.
6 I'm so tired. Our P.E. teacher .... us run for an hour!
7 My parents won't .... me to miss any school unless I'm sick.
8 I can't drink coffee. It .... me stay up all night.

5 **Read the rules and complete the speech bubbles with the correct form of *make, let, allow,* or *not allow.***

Welcome to the **Life in the Middle Ages** weekend! To discover how people lived long ago, there are certain rules we have to follow:

1 No electronic games, since they weren't even invented then!
2 No makeup.
3 No cell phones, but you can use the pay phone in the reception area.
4 No radios. Entertainment in the Middle Ages included acting and singing and dancing. So get ready to entertain us!
5 No showers, although you may take a bath.
6 No single rooms. We have to share, four to a tent.

1 They didn't .... me play my computer game!

2 We weren't .... to wear makeup.

3 They didn't .... us to use cell phones. But they .... us use the pay phone.

4 They didn't .... us listen to radios. They .... us sing, act, and dance!

5 We weren't .... to use the shower, but we were .... to take a bath.

6 They .... us share tents.

6 **Write sentences about these signs. Use *(not) allow* and the verbs below.**

dive   eat and drink   park   ride your bike

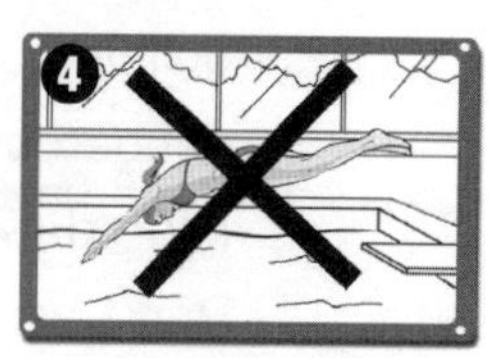

1 You .... in the auditorium.
2 You .... here.
3 You .... for one hour.
4 You .... here.

Skills

Reading

1. **Read the description below quickly. What kind of text is it?**

a) an email b) a blog c) a magazine article

Tom Wilkinson

MONDAY, July 6

As most of you know, I don't like running. I never go jogging, and I wouldn't run a marathon even if I was paid for it. But one thing that would make me run for my life, literally, would be if there were several hundred bulls chasing me.

Tomorrow, that's exactly what people are coming here to do. I'm at the annual San Fermin Fiesta in Pamplona, Spain.

This festival began in the Middle Ages, and has grown in popularity ever since. It lasts for a week in July, when the city is transformed into an ocean of red and white, the official colors of the festival.

Before the bullring was built, bull fights were held in a large square in the city. The custom of running ahead of the bulls started when the bulls had to be moved from the outskirts of the city to the bullring. Some of the customs have changed over the years, but certain things are still the same.

Anyone who wants to participate in the run has to enter the special area by 7:30 a.m. The gates are then closed, and they won't be opened to let you leave after that. At just before 8:00 a.m. the runners ask the statue of San Fermin to protect them. At eight o'clock, two rockets are fired. With the first rocket, the gates of the bull enclosure are opened, and with the second, the bulls are set free to run. They chase after the runners down the length of the bull run, which is about 800 meters. The whole thing lasts about two minutes.

It sounds easier than it is. You can't just run straight ahead. The route goes up and down narrow streets, with few places for runners to hide except doorways of buildings. The end of the run, just before the bulls enter the ring, is one of the most dangerous spots. People running with the bulls have fallen here, and have been injured (sometimes fatally).

Don't worry if you're reading this, Mom. No one under the age of 18 is allowed to participate. I'll be watching from the safety of the balcony!

2 **Circle T (True) or F (False) for the sentences below. Correct the false sentences.**

1 Tom has gone to Pamplona to run in the fiesta. T / F

....

2 The fiesta is a lot more than 100 years old. T / F ....

3 The fiesta starts on July 7. T / F ....

4 Once you have decided to run in the fiesta, you aren't allowed to change your mind. T / F

....

5 There are many places to hide from the bulls in the narrow streets. T / F

....

6 The race gets easier toward the end. T / F ....

7 Anyone can take part. T / F ....

8 Tom knows his mother might be reading this blog. T / F ....

3 **Find words in the blog that mean:**

1 a race of about 42 km ....

2 changed ....

3 legally recognized and allowed ....

4 edges ....

5 traditions ....

6 fenced area ....

7 in a deadly way ....

8 take part ....

Listening

24 **4** **Listen to Part 1. Where is the speaker?**

a) a music festival b) a fashion show c) a school fair d) a sports event

25 **5** **Listen to Part 2 and answer the questions.**

1 Where is the event held? ....

2 Where is the speaker staying? ....

3 How did he get a ticket? ....

4 What did his parents want him to do instead? ....

5 Why did they let him go eventually? ....

Writing for your Portfolio

6 **Write a short description of an event you have been to.**

- What kind of event was it?
- When and where was it held?
- What did you do there?
- What was it like?

UNIT 7 Food, glorious food

26 **1 Complete the dialogue using the words below. There are two words you won't use. Then listen and check.**

don't are aren't 'll do raw guess fried

Jack What are you doing tonight, Molly?
Molly Nothing special. Why?
Jack Let's go out to a Mexican restaurant. I [1]........................ pay.
Molly That's very sweet, but I don't really like Mexican food.
Jack Really. Why not?
Molly I don't like spicy food.
Jack OK. What about Japanese? You like sushi, [2]........................ you?
Molly Well, not really. I don't like [3]........................ fish.
Jack Well, you could have a noodle dish. Noodles with [4]........................ chicken, or something like that.
Molly Noodles? No thanks.
Jack I give up.
Molly I'm sorry. You're not mad at me, [5]........................ you?
Jack I [6]........................ not. I suppose I'll just go by myself.

2 Circle T (True) or F (False) for the sentences below.

1 Jack invites Molly out to eat. T / F
2 Molly wants to share the cost. T / F
3 Molly doesn't like hot food. T / F
4 Molly prefers cooked fish. T / F
5 Molly loves noodles. T / F
6 Jack is angry with Molly. T / F

Making offers

3 Match the suggestions and offers.

1 Let's get a DVD to watch tonight.
2 Let's have a glass of juice.
3 Let's have something to eat.
4 Let's have a party.
5 Let's invite Paul.
6 Let's get Mom a present.

a) OK. I'll make some sandwiches.
b) I'll get some paper so we can make a list of what to do.
c) Great. I'll get a comedy on the way home from school.
d) Yes. I'll call him tonight.
e) Yes, let's get her some flowers.
f) Good idea. I'll get some glasses.

4 Write an offer under each of the pictures.

Example Let me help you. 1 .... 2 .... 3 ....

Language Focus

Vocabulary Food

1 Find 12 food words in the grid and write them in the correct columns. Look in all directions.

1 Ways of serving food

....

....

....

2 Words to describe taste

....

....

....

S	R	O	A	S	T	E	D
T	S	I	K	A	L	Y	T
F	B	M	C	F	W	A	R
R	O	I	H	H	S	R	U
I	I	L	O	R	T	M	O
E	L	D	T	E	E	W	S
D	E	K	A	B	O	A	W
Z	D	E	L	I	G	H	T
X	D	E	L	L	I	R	G

2 Use the words in Exercise 1 to complete the menus.

Looking for a fresh start to the day? Why not choose one of our menus specially designed to give you all the energy you need to get through the morning.

Morning Motivator

1.......................... eggs, bacon, and toast with 2.......................... jam. Ground 3.......................... coffee and juice will quench your thirst. A healthy way to get you up and on the move.

Winter Warmer

A large muffin, 4.......................... to perfection and served with two 5.......................... eggs and 6.......................... sausages. Perfect to get you up and at 'em on a cold winter's morning.

Talking about food

3 Use the words in Exercises 1 and 2 to complete the sentences.

1 Be careful. The chili is very .... You'll need to drink a lot of water with it.

2 I don't know how you can eat so much white chocolate. Don't you think it's ....?

3 Try this pear. It's delicious. It's so ....

4 Don't use that milk. It's probably .... It's been out on the counter all day.

5 I don't like spicy food, but I can eat foods that are ....

6 The cake is delicious. It's incredibly .... and fluffy.

Grammar

Will / won't Predictions

1 Write the number of the correct sentence next to the picture.

1 I think number 13 will win.
2 Number 13 won't win now.
3 Be careful. It'll be very cold.
4 Be careful. It'll be hot.
5 Don't get too close. It'll bite you.
6 Don't be afraid. It won't bite you.
7 Don't buy it now. It'll be cheaper next week.
8 Buy it now. There won't be any left soon.

2 Complete the dialogues with *'ll* or *won't*.

1 **A** I'm really worried about my French test tomorrow.
B Don't worry. You .... be fine. You're really good at French.
A Thanks, but I'm nervous. I .... be able to fall asleep tonight.
B Drink a glass of warm milk and you .... be asleep in minutes.

2 **A** If you don't finish your lunch, you .... get hungry before dinner.
B No, I .... I had a big breakfast.
A But that .... keep you going until this evening.
B Well, if I get hungry I .... have a bag of chips or string cheese.
A Well, that's not very healthy, is it?

3 **A** Who do you think .... win the championship this year?
B I'm not sure, but it definitely .... be us. We're playing terribly.
A What about North High? They're playing well.
B Yeah but Lane High is really good. I think they .... beat them this week.

4 **A** We're going on vacation tomorrow so we .... see you for a week.
B That's right. You're going to Florida, aren't you? I'm sure the weather .... be nice.
A I hope so. I'm sick of all this rain.
B And when you get back, it .... almost be summer. Sun every day!
A I hope so.

Question tags (review)

3 Circle the correct word.

1 You know Charlie, *do/don't/won't* you?
2 They're going to win, *won't/aren't/are* they?
3 You didn't say anything, *did/didn't/don't* you?
4 I'm right, *wasn't/aren't/isn't* I?
5 That test wasn't easy, *was/wasn't/were* it?
6 The Westwoods don't have a car, *don't/do/aren't* they?
7 It'll rain this afternoon, *will/is/won't* it?
8 She loved the movie, *didn't/wasn't/doesn't* she?

4 Match the sentences with the tags.

1	She doesn't like me,	a)	will you?
2	I'm not late,	b)	aren't they?
3	You won't tell anyone,	c)	didn't he?
4	Paul lives near you,	d)	isn't it?
5	Mom and Dad are going out tonight,	e)	does she?
6	Mrs Green didn't give us any homework,	f)	was she?
7	Tom told you about my party,	g)	am I?
8	It's cold today,	h)	don't you?
9	You eat meat,	i)	did she?
10	She wasn't happy,	j)	doesn't he?

27 ### 5 Match the food with the country. Then listen and check.

the food quiz

1	Chow mein	a)	Japan
2	Sushi	b)	India
3	Samosas	c)	Italy
4	Gorgonzola	d)	Mexico
5	Tortillas	e)	China

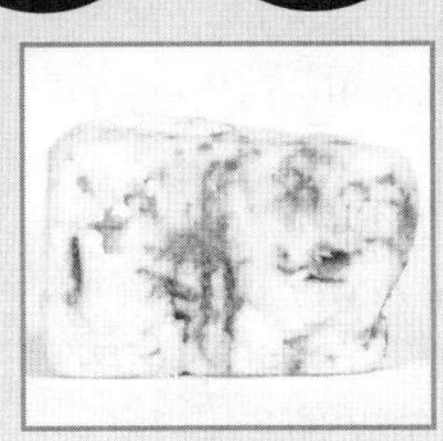
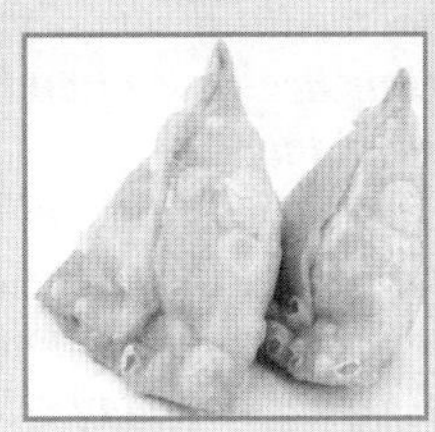

6 Complete with the correct question tags.

1 Stir-fry is Chinese, ...?
2 You went to Beijing last year, ...?
3 We were right, ...?
4 Sushi was invented by the Japanese, ...?
5 The Japanese are famous for eating raw fish, ...?
6 Samosas aren't Indian, ...?
7 You don't like Indian food, ...?
8 Gorgonzola. That sounds Italian, ...?

Skills

Reading

1 Read the article and answer the questions.

1 How much fruit and vegetables should teenage boys eat every day?
2 What disease can a healthy diet of fruit and vegetables help prevent?
3 How else are fruit and vegetables good for us?
4 Why is it important for children to eat a good diet?
5 Which child/children think(s):
   a) there's no problem eating things like hamburgers and french fries sometimes?
   b) being active is more important than a healthy diet?
   c) moms and dads should make sure their children eat well?
   d) a bad diet could lead to an early death?
   e) the way you feel is more important than what you eat?

Why eat more fruit and vegetables?

Fruit and vegetables are important in a healthy diet. Doctors now recommend that teenage girls eat four cups and boys eat five cups of fruit and vegetables a day. There are many advantages to eating fruit and vegetables:
-They help reduce the causes of heart disease.
-They protect against many cancers.
-They provide a lot of energy.
-They keep skin, teeth, and hair healthy.
-They protect against asthma.

The way we think about food and how it affects our health is often heavily influenced by our childhood.
If we can get kids to form healthy habits early on in life, they have a better chance of staying healthy throughout the rest of their lives. So what do today's teenagers think? We asked a few for their opinions.

"It's OK to eat junk food two or three times a week, but you shouldn't eat it every day. You should try and have healthy meals the other days."
Daniel, 14, Atlanta, Georgia

"Of course it's important how much you weigh. If you weigh more than you should, you're putting pressure on your heart and you could end up killing yourself. It's important to watch what you eat."
Kyle, 13, Springfield, Illinois

"The most important thing is to be happy. If you can be happy eating healthy food, then that's great. I like to eat fruit and vegetables, but I couldn't live without candy and chocolate. I'd just be too unhappy."
Lucy, 15, Nashville, Tennessee

"I don't think food is the biggest problem when you're young. I think exercise is much more important. If you do a lot of exercise, you can eat what you want."
Shireen, 14, Richmond, Virginia

"I think parents have to be responsible for their children. I know it's not always easy, but they have to make sure we eat healthy food."
Kirsty, 16, Milwaukee, Wisconsin

Writing

2 Write a paragraph about healthy eating.

Reading and listening

3 **Read the article and circle T (True) or F (False).**

1 An average British person eats 4kg of candy more each year than an Irish person. T / F
2 About half of all candy Americans eat is chocolate. T / F
3 The Swiss eat more candy than the British. T / F
4 Chocolate started out as a drink. T / F
5 In the 1920s, there were 40,000 different kinds of candy bars. T / F

Every year, Americans eat 7 billion tons of candy. That's about 10 kilograms of candy per person, which is less than the average amount of candy eaten by Europeans. In Europe, the Swiss eat the most candy, followed by the UK, where the average person eats 14kg of candy each year. In Ireland, the average person eats 11kg, and in Germany 10kg.

About half of all the candy consumed by Americans is chocolate, but most people don't know that chocolate started out as a drink. In fact, Montezuma, emperor of the Aztecs, drank chocolate. Hernando Cortez brought chocolate back to Spain in 1529, but it wasn't until 1875 that milk chocolate was first made and paved the way for the candy bar. Milton S. Hershey produced his first chocolate bars in 1894 and other Americans began making their own candy bar recipes. By the 1920s, as many as 40,000 different candy bars were available.

28 **4** **Listen to the story about *The Food Dudes* and write the name of the character under the food they like best.**

1 ....

2 ....

3 ....

4 ....

Tom
Rocco
Raz
Charlie

29 **5** **Listen again and circle the correct answer.**

1 When was the *Popeye* cartoon made?
a) In the 1930s b) In the 1940s c) In the 1950s

2 How much did sales of spinach rise because of *Popeye*?
a) by 30% b) by 33% c) by 37%

3 Who is the Food Dudes' enemy?
a) General Pizza b) General Punk c) General Junk

4 What age range is *The Food Dudes* show aimed at?
a) 4–7 b) 4–11 c) 7–11

5 What else does *The Food Dudes* show offer?
a) stickers and pencils for teachers
b) free fruit and vegetables for kids and teachers
c) help for teachers in the classroom

UNIT 8 Body talk

1 **Read the article and write the name of the correct country under the pictures.**

1 ....

2 ....

3 ....

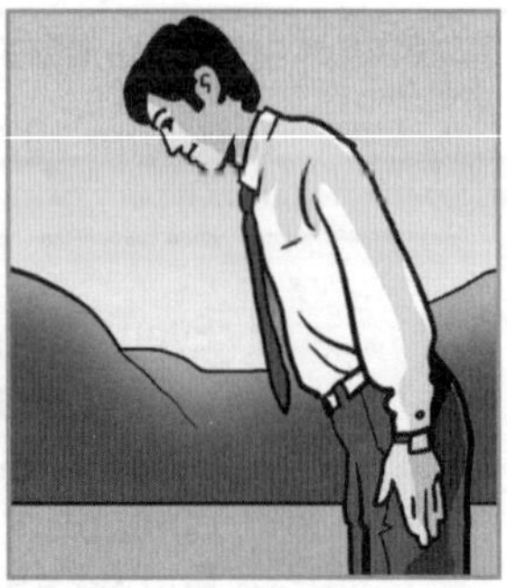

4 ....

Say hello

Some of us shake hands, some kiss or hug. Others just say "hello." These ways of greeting may be common in Europe and the Americas, but they don't mean much in other countries around the world. Take a trip around Asia, for example. Here are some of the ways of greeting you'd probably have to learn if you lived there:

With 1.3 billion inhabitants, China has the world's largest population, so let's start there. Many Chinese people say "hi" with a simple nod of the head, but older Chinese people put their hands together, fingers between fingers, in front of their throat and then nod. This technique is also commonly used in Hong Kong.

After China, India is the world's most populated country with 1.1 billion people. India is famous for its traditional way of saying "hello" known as the Namaste. To do the Namaste you need to put the palms of your hands together in front of you and then nod or bend the upper part of your body a little.

In Japan you slightly bow from the waist by bending the upper part of your body forward. At the same time, you need to keep the palms of your hands on the fronts of your legs and keep your feet together.

Greeting others is a little easier in Indonesia. You don't need to learn any complicated body movement. Just remember the word *selamat* and say it whenever you meet someone. *Selamat* means "peace."

If you want something more difficult, then try the Malaysian greeting. When you meet a friend use both your hands to touch the other person's hands. Then take your hands away and put them on your chest. This is called the *salam* gesture and it needs a little practice.

2 **Read again and answer the questions with the name(s) of a country/countries.**

Which country's greeting involves ...

1 the upper part of the body? ....

2 the upper and lower parts of the body? ....

3 physical contact? ....

4 the head? ....

5 speaking? ....

3 **How do you greet different people? Write a short description.**

Language Focus

Vocabulary Body movements

1 **How do you think these people are feeling? Write the emotion under the picture.**

excited	bored	confused	angry	interested

1 He's ....

2 She's ....

3 She's ....

4 He's ....

5 He's ....

Talking about body movements

2 **Look at the pictures from Exercise 1 and complete the sentences using the words below.**

crossed	shook	pointed	frowned
nodding	scratched	folded	waving

1 Antonio looked at the exam. He was confused. He .... his head and .... This was a history test, wasn't it? So why were all the questions in French?
2 Donna works as a reporter for her local newspaper. She goes to hear the mayor speak and stands there .... her head to everything he says.
3 Janet was so excited. She hadn't seen her best friend Andrea for more than a year. The train arrived and Janet jumped up and down on the platform .... her hands.
4 Steve didn't want to be there. He didn't really like football and he was bored. He .... his legs, ... his arms and looked at his watch. Another 40 minutes to go.
5 The scoutmaster was angry. Two of the scouts had wandered off and became lost. He.................................. his finger at the Larkin boys when he saw them. They .... their heads. "It wasn't our fault," they said.

3 **What body movements do you make when you are excited, bored, tired, etc.? Choose some of the emotions below and write about your body movements.**

relaxed	angry	confused	excited	interested
disappointed	scared	happy	bored	tired

When I'm angry with my sister, I fold my arms and frown at her.

Grammar

Could, might, may for speculation

1 Look at the pictures and complete the sentences using the words below.

could hit | may need | might bite | could miss | might lose

1 What are you doing? It ....

2 Think positive. He ....

3 Be careful. You .... your head.

4 Don't worry! She .... them.

5 Don't forget your umbrella. You .... it.

2 How much do you know about the world's different languages? Look at the words below and decide which language they are. Choose from the words in the box and write sentences.

Greek | Hebrew | Japanese | Chinese | Arabic | Korean | German | Portuguese

❶ 涑 ❷ 房子 ❸ 집

❹ σπίτι ❺ בֶּגֶד ❻ Haus

❼ Roupa ❽ ملابس

1 *It may be Japanese.*
2 ....
3 ....
4 ....
5 ....
6 ....
7 ....
8 ....

30 **3 Now listen and check. How well did you do?**

4 Rewrite the sentences to include the word in parentheses.

Don't pet the dog. It's possible it bites. (could)
Don't pet the dog. It could bite.

1 It's possibly the best movie I've ever seen. (might)
....
....

2 Don't eat that mushroom. It's possibly poisonous. (could)
....
....

3 It looks bad. Your leg is possibly broken. (might)
....
....

–ed vs. *–ing* adjectives

5 Look at the pictures and put a check next to the correct sentences.

☐ The children are frightened.
☐ The children are frightening.

☐ The acrobats are amazing.
☐ The acrobats are amazed.

☐ Bob is worried.
☐ Bob is worrying.

☐ The children are fascinated.
☐ The children are fascinating.

☐ Dawn is disappointed.
☐ Dawn is disappointing.

☐ Mr. White is bored.
☐ Mr. White is boring.

6 Complete the sentences using the words below.

excited	tired	insulted	frightened
exciting	tiring	insulting	frightening

1 Dad was so .... he almost fell asleep during the movie.
2 Do you find it .... when people ask you how old you are?
3 It was Eve's birthday and she was so .... she couldn't stop giggling.
4 I was all alone in the dark and then I heard a scream. I've never been so ....
5 My sister's going to have a baby. It's the most .... news of the year. I'm so happy.
6 The movie was so .... I had to close my eyes several times.
7 It was such a .... day that all I wanted to do was go home and go to bed.
8 He was so rude to me. I've never been so .... in my life.

7 Read the beginnings of the sentences and circle the correct word.

1 The most *bored/boring* day of the week is ....
2 I'm not very *interested/interesting* in ....
3 The subject I find most *fascinated/fascinating* in school is ....
4 The most *excited/exciting* day of my life was ....
5 The time of day when I feel most *tired/tiring* is ....
6 The most *disappointing/disappointed* grade I got was ....
7 I get really *frightened/frightening* when ....
8 I'm most *worried/worrying* about ....

8 Now complete the sentences about yourself.

Skills

Reading

1 Complete the sentences using the words from the box.

holds | smallest | drinks | grow | stronger | takes | body | born

Nails

Your fingernails [1].............................. four times as fast as your toenails.

It [2].............................. around six months to grow a new nail.

Lee Redmond stopped cutting her nails in 1979. She [3].............................. the record for the longest fingernails in the world. Their total length was more than 7.5 meters, but she lost her nails in a car crash in 2009.

Bones

Babies are [4].............................. with 300 bones. Adults only have 206.

Bones are four times [5].............................. than concrete.

The [6].............................. bone in your body is in your ears.

Water

The human [7].............................. is 75 percent water.

An average person [8].............................. around 73,000 liters of water in his or her lifetime.

Listening

31 **2 Listen to the radio show and write the correct names under the photos.**

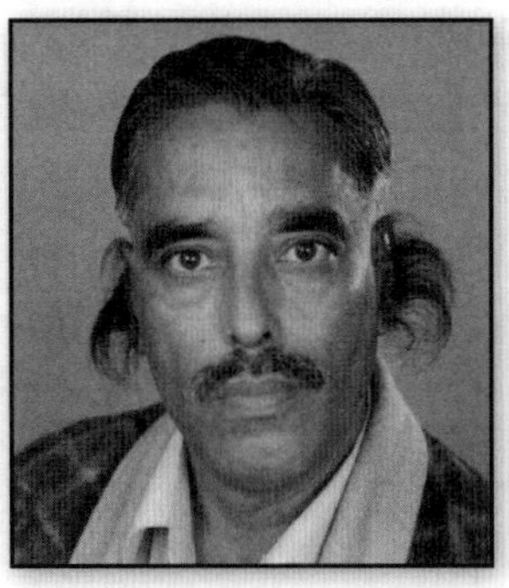

Xie Qiuping

Radhakant Bajpal

Leonid Stadnik

....

32 **3 Listen again and circle T (True) or F (False) for the sentences below.**

1 Your arm span is the same distance as your height. T / F
2 At 2.57 meters, Leonid Stadnyk from the Ukraine is the world's tallest man. T / F
3 People grow during the night. T / F
4 Chimpanzees have more hair than humans. T / F
5 Most people have around 100,000 hairs on their head. T / F
6 Xie Qiuping from China has the longest hair. It is 5.627 meters long. T / F
7 She has been growing it since she was 30. T / F
8 Radhakant Bajpai from Egypt holds the record for the longest ear hair. T / F

Reading

4 **Read the magazine article and answer the questions.**

Many teenagers are choosing to have their noses or other parts of their bodies pierced these days. Their parents often don't understand, and this can create problems in the family home. But who is right? Should adults accept that things have changed from when they were young, or do mom and dad know best? We asked you to tell us what you think.

Pretty much all the girls in my school have pierced ears, that's no problem. But pierced noses are different. There aren't many students with pierced noses at my school so there's no pressure to do it. I think if a teenager wants to do it because he or she likes the way it looks, they should be able to.
Sally, 17

When they are 18 and leave home, my kids can do what they want to. Until then, they live in my house and have to obey my rules. One of my rules is definitely no piercings. So far there hasn't been a problem. I hope it stays that way.
James, 50

My school doesn't allow students to have pierced noses so it doesn't really matter what my mom and dad think because my school has already made the decision for me.
Karima, 16

When I was a teenager I fought with my mom and dad because I wanted to get my ear pierced. In the end I waited until I left home and went to college. I haven't worn an earring for years now. If my children ask me if they can get their nose pierced, I'll try to help them see why it's better to wait, but if they really want to do it, it will be difficult to say no.
Trevor, 45

It's a fashion and, like most fashions, it really doesn't matter. What's the big deal? There are far more important things in the world to worry about.
Dawn, 34

Who....

1 thinks piercing's not an important issue? ....
2 pierced their ear to prove a point? ....
3 definitely doesn't want their children to get nose piercings? ....
4 doesn't feel under any pressure to get her nose pierced? ....
5 would prefer their children to wait before making a decision about getting a nose piercing? ....
6 thinks teenagers should be able to look the way they want to? ....
7 definitely won't stop their children if they want a nose piercing? ....
8 goes to a school with a ban on wearing nose rings? ....

Writing for your Portfolio

5 **What do you think about nose piercing? Write a short letter to the magazine explaining your feelings.**

UNIT 9 Fame

33 **1 Number the lines in the correct order. Then listen and check.**

Simon .... No way. William H. Macy is definitely going to win that.
Simon .... Don't bother. You can borrow my copy. In fact, why don't you come over tonight and watch it with me?
Simon .....1...... Who do you think is going to win the Oscars?
Simon .... He's that actor who was in *Mystery Men.*
Simon .... You've never seen it? It's the funniest movie ever made.
Kate .... I've never seen it.
Kate .... That sounds fun.
Kate .... OK, I'll get a copy from the DVD place.
Kate .... I'm not sure. Maybe Tom Cruise will win best actor.
Kate .... William H. Macy? Who's he?

2 Circle T (True) or F (False) for the sentences below.

1 Kate thinks Tom Cruise might get the Oscar for best actor. T / F
2 Tom Cruise was the actor in *Mystery Men.* T / F
3 Simon liked the movie *Mystery Men.* T / F
4 Kate has never seen *Mystery Men.* T / F
5 Simon has the DVD of *Mystery Men.* T / F
6 Kate doesn't want to watch the movie tonight with Simon. T / F

Talking about past and present favorites

3 Match the questions and answers.

1 Who's your favorite singer?
2 What's your favorite hobby?
3 Who's your favorite actress?
4 What was your favorite food when you were a kid?
5 What's your favorite food now?

a) Well, I used to love banana sandwiches. Can you believe it?
b) It's probably Beyoncé! I love her songs.
c) Mushroom pizza. It's strange, I hated it when I was a kid!
d) Scarlett Johansson! She was great in her last movie.
e) Well, I used to like playing computer games, but now I prefer reading.

4 Write sentences about these people.

	2006	Now	
Example: Kate	~~Jennifer Aniston~~	Sandra Bullock	Kate used to like Jennifer Aniston, but now she likes Sandra Bullock.
1 Martin	~~Scissor Sisters~~	The Rolling Stones	....
2 Pam	~~hamburgers~~	burritos	....
3 Eddie	~~Brad Pitt~~	Ben Stiller	....

Language Focus

Vocabulary Award shows

1 Complete the sentences using the words below.

picture	actress	solo female artist	animated movie	actor
single	group	solo male artist	album	

1 And the award for best .... goes to Johnny Depp.

2 And the award for best .... goes to Kanye West.

3 And the award for best .... goes to Beyoncé.

4 And the award for best .... goes to *Happy Feet.*

5 And the award for best .... goes to Scarlett Johansson.

6 And the award for best .... goes to The Rolling Stones.

7 And the award for best .... of all time goes to *Yesterday* by The Beatles.

8 And the award for best .... goes to *International Super Hits* by Green Day.

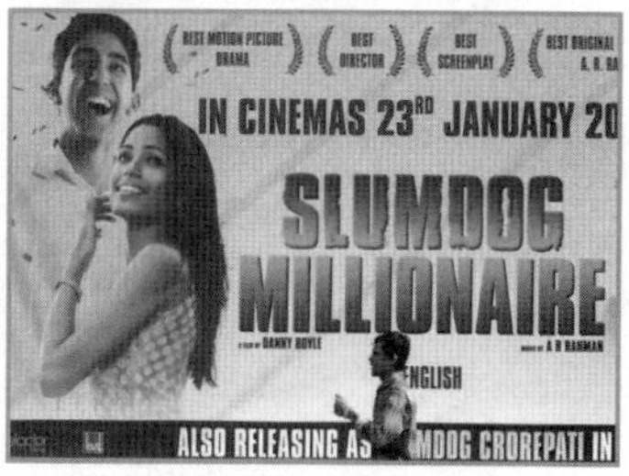

9 And the award for best .... goes to *Slumdog Millionaire.*

2 Complete these sentences. Choose five categories. Write the names of the categories and your winners.

My awards for this year!

1 Award for best .... goes to ....
2 Award for best .... goes to ....
3 Award for best .... goes to ....
4 Award for best .... goes to ....
5 Award for best .... goes to ....

Grammar

Used to

1 Reorder the words and write complete sentences.

1 used / We / pizza / every / have / night / Saturday / to

....

2 watch / He / to / use / didn't / football ....

3 live / in / My / used / parents / to / Tokyo ....

4 use / I / to / fruit / eat / didn't ....

5 to / like / use / our / I / neighbors / didn't ....

6 father / use / Did / your / band / to / in / a / play ? ....

2 Complete the sentences using the phrases below.

used to argue	didn't use to like	used to go
used to work	didn't use to have	didn't use to speak

1 We .... to the movie theater every weekend, but now it's closed down.

2 My sister and I .... all the time, but now we're good friends.

3 I .... my own bedroom, but now we live in a bigger house and I don't have to share.

4 I .... vegetables, but now I eat them all the time.

5 I .... French, but now I can say a lot of things.

6 My father .... in a bank, but now he's a writer.

3 Complete each sentence with a verb in the simple present and a verb with *used to.*

1 She .... (dance) a lot when she was young, but now she .... (not dance) at all.

2 These days we .... (not go) to the park, but we .... (go) every weekend.

3 That building .... (be) a restaurant now, but it .... (be) a bookstore.

4 My mother.................... (not work) now, but she .... (work) for the government.

5 When I was young, I .... (not wear) sneakers, but now I .... (wear) them all the time.

4 Write sentences about Sally.

Example: Sally used to like salad, but now she likes pizza.

1 (job) ....

2 (work) ....

3 (hair) ....

4 (sports) ....

5 (home) ....

Gerunds after prepositions

5 **Complete the sentences using the prepositions below.**

at in into on of to

1 I like playing football but I'm not very good .... it.
2 I don't get a good grade in history because I'm not interested .... it.
3 I didn't use to like tennis but now I'm really keen .... it.
4 There's a party tomorrow night. I'm looking forward .... it.
5 She was sad when her pet gerbil died. She was very fond .... it.
6 Phil loves rock music. He's really .... it.

6 **Match the sentences and the pictures.**

1 Their father wasn't very good at cooking. ....
2 My brother's thinking of getting a new car. ....
3 She wasn't very interested in looking at cars. ....
4 Dad insisted on driving. ....
5 Jamie's fond of traveling. ....
6 They're looking forward to leaving. ....

7 **Complete the sentences with a preposition and the correct form of the verbs in parentheses.**

1 I'm not really keen .... (go) to the movies tonight.
2 She's really good .... (tell) jokes.
3 I'm thinking .... (buy) a new MP3 player.
4 Do you just like listening to music, or are you good .... (dance), too?
5 Are your parents looking forward .... (go) on vacation?
6 He's good at grammar, but he's hopeless .... (explain) it to other people.
7 Sorry, I'm just not interested .... (listen) to your problems.
8 I was enjoying the party, but my friend insisted .... (leave)

Skills

Reading

1 Read the poster. Answer the questions.

1 What kind of show is it?
2 How much does it cost to enter?
3 When will the show take place?
4 Where will the show happen?
5 What prize will the winner get?

Have you got what it takes to be the next star?

TALENT SHOW

Can you sing?
Can you play an instrument?
Are you an actor?
Can you juggle?
Do you have any other special talents?

Interested? It's simple. Fill in a form and send it with a check for $5 to Miss Davis at County Hall.
Come to the town library at 3:00 on Saturday and show us what you're made of.
You could win $500 and the chance to have your own TV show!

What are you waiting for???

Listening

34 **2 Listen to Max and Polly talking about the talent show. Circle two differences between what they say and the information in the poster.**

35 **3 Listen again and circle the correct answers.**

1 What's the name of Polly's dog?
a) Spot b) Fido c) Lucky

2 What's Polly's act?

3 What does Max play in the band?
a) the guitar b) the drums c) the keyboard

4 What's Max's act?

Writing

4 **Read the review of Polly's performance and complete it using the words below.**

incredible Spot legs hoops check talented

Polly and her dog [1]...................... gave the best performance of the talent show. Spot really is a [2]...................... dog. The way he walked on two [3]...................... was amazing. He was just like a human. But the highlight of the show was when he jumped through the [4]...................... that were on fire. It was [5]...................... They really deserved the $500 [6]...................... that they won. I look forward to seeing their TV show.

5 **Use your imagination and write a short review of Max's act.**

Reading

6 **Read the chat page and answer the questions.**

We asked you if you'd like to be famous. Here's what you told us.

I'd love to be famous. It would be so great to be in a successful band. I could travel around the world and see all the places that I've always dreamed of. And you wouldn't have to do anything, someone would do it all for you. I'd only fly first class and stay in five-star hotels. I'd also get to meet a lot of interesting people and hang out with other famous people. It must be great never having to worry about money and buying everything you want. I'd give a lot of it to charities, too. It would be good to use your influence to make things better for other people.

Paul from Sacramento

I'd like to be respected by the people around me. If this makes me famous then that's great but if it doesn't, it's no big deal. I write poetry. I'm a member of a poetry club and sometimes we read our poems to one another. It's a great feeling when people hear your poems and like them. It makes you feel good. I've even had some poems printed in my local newspaper. That was a great experience. Not many people become famous writing poems, so I really don't expect much. It would be amazing just to make a living writing poetry. I'd be happy with that.

Julie from Omaha

I'd hate to be famous. The money would be nice, but it's too high a price for losing your privacy. Imagine never being able to go anywhere without hundreds of photographers following you everywhere. That would be a nightmare. These days there are far too many people who are famous for doing nothing. This is because of shows such as *Big Brother*. They take ordinary people and try to make them special. They're not special. They're just ordinary like you and me. Why do people think they are interesting? I don't understand.

Harry from St. Louis

Who…

1 thinks being able to live your own life is more important than being famous? ....
2 would spend a lot of money if they were famous? ....
3 would like to go to a lot of different places? ....
4 likes it when other people show their appreciation? ....
5 doesn't think they'll become famous? ....
6 thinks reality TV is making people with no talent famous? ....
7 would like to help other people? ....
8 is a writer? ....

UNIT 10 Crazy collections

A

1 **Read the descriptions and match them to the correct photo.**

B

1 At the age of 14, Roy H. often helped his father, who was a carpenter. His job was to sort out the nails, and soon Roy began collecting them. Amazingly, he now has more than 15,000 different kinds of nails from more than 40 countries. All the nails are added to a long list and kept in the basement of his house. It is the most complete collection of its kind in existence.

Not surprisingly, Roy is very proud of some very special nails: The 50 nails which came from U.S. state capitol buildings, each one with a letter from the state governor. Another special nail is one from the home of William Ellery, who was one of the people who signed the Declaration of Independence.

2 David Morgan's life is devoted to traffic cones. So are his yard and garage. He has more than 500 cones in and around his home. Mr. Morgan works for a company that makes cones, and he is fascinated by the different designs.

He started his collection in 1986 and hasn't been able to stop. His favorite is a rubber cone that was made in 1956, which is the oldest item in the collection.

What does his wife, Brenda, think of his unusual hobby? David says: "She's used to it. I've been collecting them since she met me, so it's just normal for her."

His daughter Poppy says: "It's a superb collection and so unusual. I've certainly never heard of anyone else collecting traffic cones."

2 **Read the descriptions again. Write *David* or *Roy*. Which collector ...**

1 has a record of all the things in his collection? ....
2 keeps things from the collection in his yard? ....
3 keeps things from his collection in the underground part of his house? ....
4 is very proud of one thing in his collection? ....
5 is very proud of 50 things in his collection? ....
6 started his collection when he worked with his father? ....
7 started his collection when he worked for a company? ....
8 has someone in his family who thinks his collection is great? ....

3 **Read the sentences and write T (True), F (False), or DK (Don't Know—information not in text**

1 Roy H.'s father made nails. ....
2 No one has a better collection of nails than Roy H. ....
3 Roy H. asked state governors to give him nails from capitol buildings ....
4 David Morgan lives in the U.S. ....
5 The oldest item in David's collection is his favorite ....
6 David is the only person in the world who collects traffic cones ....

4 **Which of the two collectors do you think is more interesting? Write a paragraph to say why.**

Language Focus

Vocabulary Hobbies and pastimes

1 Reorder the letters and write complete phrases.

1 keeping a *glob* – ....
2 doing *zlepuzs* – ....
3 making *tryopet* – ....
4 *clgecotinl* things – ....
5 taking *hgotorhapps* – ....
6 making *lodems* – ....
7 *xgnifi* things – ....
8 playing *linoen mesag* – ....
9 going *dirb-chatwing* – ....

2 Write the number of the correct phrase from Exercise 1 in each picture.

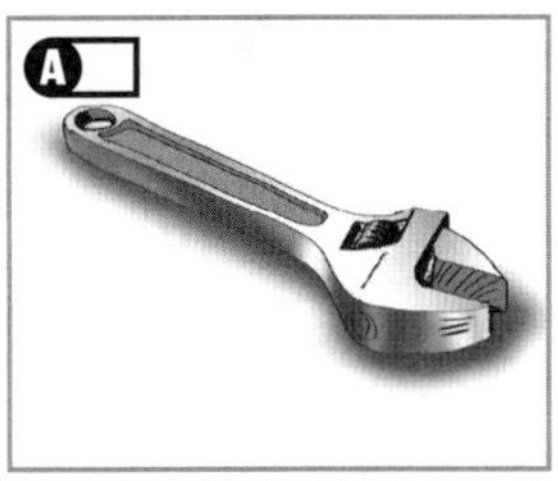

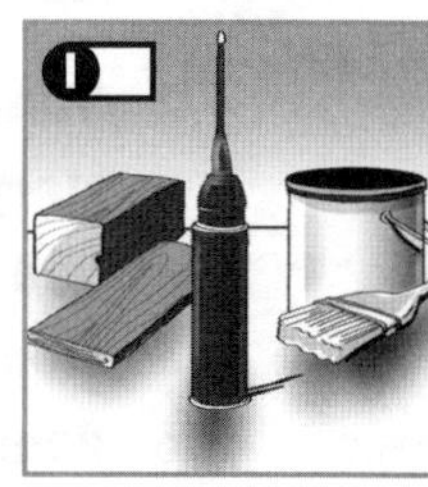

Talking about hobbies

3 Read the sentences. Write which hobby you think each person is doing.

1 "I only need two more and then I'll have the complete set." collecting things
2 "Can you see it, Peter? Look up in the tree! It has blue wings and a red beak." ....
3 "I'm almost finished. It's going to be the best plane I've ever made!" ....
4 "It's really hard to make this pot. I've been trying for an hour and it keeps breaking!" ....
5 "Can you help me? I don't know the answer to this one here." ....
6 "OK, the computer's on. Now, what shall I write about today?" ....
7 "No, that one's too dark. Let me take another one. I'll use the flash this time." ....
8 "If I can just get another 100 points, I'll have the high score." ....
9 "It's my sister's bike. The brakes are stuck. But I almost have them working again." ....

4 Write down the names of four hobbies that people you know (friends or family) like doing.

Example: My father likes fixing things.

1 ....
2 ....
3 ....
4 ....

Grammar

Present perfect continuous

1 Write the number of the correct sentence in each picture.

1 "That's really bad, Andy. You haven't been practicing enough."
2 "I haven't been feeling well since Sunday."
3 "My eyes hurt. I've been reading for hours."
4 "Come on, Jimmy! It's my turn. You've been using the computer all morning!"
5 "I'm exhausted! I've been running for more than an hour!"
6 "Come on, Marcie, let's go for a walk. We've been studying since nine o'clock."

2 Complete the dialogues. Write the verbs in parentheses in the present perfect continuous.

1 **Steve** Sorry I'm late.
Mary Steve! I .... (wait) for you for 25 minutes!
2 **Dad** Turn the TV off now, Alex.
Mom Yes, you .... (watch) TV all evening, it's time for bed now.
3 **Paul** You play the guitar really well.
Hannah Thanks. I'm better than I was. I .... (take) lessons for six weeks.
4 **Bethan** Is everything OK, Mike?
Mike Yes and no. I .... (do) my homework since seven o'clock, and I still haven't finished.
5 **Tony** Your sister's face is red.
Lynne Yes, she .... (cry) all morning.
6 **Sally** Wow, your dog's dirty, isn't it?
Martin Yeah, that's right. He .... (play) in the park.

3 Complete each sentence with a phrase below.

been doing   been cooking   been looking   been playing   been reading   been writing

1 She plays tennis really well, and she's only .... for six months.
2 I'm only on page 3 of this book, and I've .... for hours!
3 My fingers hurt. I've .... emails since three o'clock.
4 We're having a party tonight. I've .... food all afternoon.
5 I can't find my watch. I've .... for it since I got up.
6 What? You haven't finished yet? What have you .... all morning?

Embedded questions

4 **Circle the correct word.**

1 Excuse me, what time *it is / is it*?
2 I'm sorry, I don't know what *is the time / time it is.*
3 When *the store opens / does the store open*?
4 I have no idea when *it opens / does it open.*
5 Excuse me, how much *this magazine costs / does this magazine cost*?
6 I don't know how much *it costs / does it cost.*
7 How many CDs *you do have / do you have*?
8 I'm not sure how many people *I have invited / have I invited.*

5 **Look at the pictures and complete the sentences.**

1 She doesn't know ....

2 He wants to know ....

3 He doesn't know ....

4 The policeofficer wants to know ....

5 They don't know ....

6 He's wondering ....

6 **Write one sentence with an embedded question for each pair of sentences.**

1 How old is this house? I really don't know. I really don't know how old this house is.
2 Where are my friends? I want to know. ....
3 How many people are in the room? I'm not sure. ....
4 How often does the bus come? I don't know. ....
5 What do you mean? I have no idea. ....
6 What time does the train arrive? I'd like to know. ....

Skills

Reading

1 **Read the article quickly. What does the writer collect?**

a) concert tickets b) autographs c) tennis balls

2 **Read the article again. Number the pictures in the correct order.**

How my collection started (by Annie Jacobs)

How did my collection start? Well, it was about five years ago, I was 12 years old, and I was getting interested in sports, especially tennis. My dad wanted to encourage me, so he took me to the tennis court near our apartment. We used to spend two or three hours sometimes, just hitting balls over the net. But then one day I said to him: "Dad, this is a lot of fun, but you know, I'd really like to see some top-class players." So Dad bought tickets that year for us to go to a top tennis competition–the U.S. Open! The first match we saw was just OK, but then we went to another court and we were so lucky–it was a match with Roger Federer! He won, of course, and at the end of the match, he threw a tennis ball up into the crowd–and I caught it! I was so excited. I tried to get close to the exit, and as he was leaving the court, I said to him: "Thanks for the tennis ball, can you sign it please?" And he did! I showed it the next day to some of my friends and they thought it was amazing. My friend James said, "I'll give you twenty bucks for that ball." Of course, I didn't sell it to him, but it started me thinking. And that was how it all started. A few weeks later, my dad took me and my friend Bella to our first concert. At, the end I waited near the back door of the auditorium, and as Gwen Stefani left I got her to sign my ticket stub! So now I had two autographs, the tennis ball and the ticket. My collection had started, and since then I've been collecting more and more autographs!

I've got about 100 now. I've got some signed photos, and some signed pieces of paper, from all kinds of famous people–sports stars, actors, singers–you name it, I've got it!

Which one's my favorite? Well, to be honest, it's still the tennis ball, my first autograph, and it's Roger Federer's!

3 **Circle T (True) or F (False) for the sentences below.**

1 Annie started playing tennis when she was 10. T / F
2 She used to play with her mother. T / F
3 The first match she saw was at the U.S. Open. T / F
4 Roger Federer signed a tennis ball for Annie. T / F
5 One of Annie's friends wanted to buy the ball. T / F
6 Annie's second autograph was from a football player. T / F
7 Now Annie has about 50 autographs. T / F
8 Her favorite autograph is Federer's. T / F

Listening

36 **4 Listen to Martin and Sarah talking about collecting stamps. Answer the questions.**

1 How did Martin start collecting stamps?
2 Why does he like collecting them?
3 What does Sarah have in her room?

37 **5 Listen again and circle T (True) or F (False) for the sentences below.**

1 Sarah has a letter from a friend in Australia. T / F
2 Sarah always knew that Martin collects stamps. T / F
3 Both Sarah and Martin have grandfathers who collect stamps. T / F
4 Martin started collecting when he was nine years old. T / F
5 Martin's stamps are mostly from Thailand and Hong Kong. T / F
6 Martin thinks it's good to have a hobby like stamp collecting. T / F
7 Martin doesn't buy stamps. T / F
8 Martin only has one stamp album. T / F

Reading

6 Read the tips and circle the correct word.

Stamp Collection Tips

You don't [1]......................... a lot of money to start a stamp collection. Perhaps you really want to start [2]......................... stamps as a hobby, but you don't want to [3]......................... a lot of money? OK, then just begin by collecting used stamps.
A [4]......................... place to start is your own mail. Of course you will probably find the same stamps again and [5]......................... at the beginning, but that doesn't [6].......................... It's a start! Another good way to get a lot of [7]......................... stamps is to ask your friends to use more [8]......................... stamps when they send you a letter.

1	need	want	ask
2	collect	collection	collecting
3	have	spend	use
4	good	best	better
5	again	more	ever
6	care	matter	depend
7	same	different	many
8	rare	unused	unusual

Writing for your Portfolio

7 Do you think collecting things is a good thing to do as a hobby? Why or why not? Write a paragraph explaining your opinion.

UNIT 11 Speak out

38 **1 Complete the dialogue using the words below. Then listen and check.**

asked him me said spoke told what

Mandy What's the matter? You look a little sad.

Josh Yes, I have a problem.

Mandy Do you want to talk about it?

Josh Yes, but I [1]...................... I wouldn't tell anyone.

Mandy Who did you say that to?

Josh My brother. I'm going to tell you anyway, because I need some advice. Jim's been acting very strangely lately. A few days ago, I went into his room to get a CD. He borrowed it from me, but he's terrible at giving things back! While I was looking for the CD, I found a box full of cell phones. Just then Jim came into the room. He was really angry and [2]...................... me [3]...................... I was doing there. I asked [4]...................... where he got the cell phones, and he [5]...................... me it was none of my business. He warned [6]...................... that if I [7]...................... about it to anyone, he would run away from home. Now I don't know what to do. Should I tell my parents? He's obviously in trouble, and I want to help him, but I don't want him to run away!

Mandy Well, if I were you, I'd definitely tell someone. Maybe not your parents, though, but someone else, a teacher maybe, or another adult who you trust.

2 Answer the questions.

1 What does Mandy want Josh to do about his problem? ....

2 Who doesn't want Josh to tell anyone? ....

3 Why did Josh decide to tell Mandy? ....

4 What did Josh ask his brother? ....

5 What is Josh afraid will happen if he tells anyone? ....

6 What does Mandy tell Josh to do? ....

Checking what people do / explaining what you do

3 Match the questions and the answers.

1 You're on the basketball team, aren't you?

2 Can you help at the school fair next weekend?

3 Are you in the school play?

4 You haven't been to our dance class before, have you?

5 Can you play a musical instrument?

a) No, this is my first time.

b) Yes, I'm the captain this year.

c) Yes, I can help sell refreshments.

d) Yes, the piano, although I'm not very good.

e) Yes, but I only come on in the last scene.

Language Focus

Vocabulary Personality adjectives

1 Circle the best adjective to describe the speakers.

I don't judge anyone. We're all different and all the same.

1 *adventurous / tolerant*

I don't like everyone looking at me. I'd rather be in the background.

2 *shy / responsible*

I care about others. I want to help everyone.

3 *negative / considerate*

My feelings are easily hurt.

4 *insensitive / sensitive*

I try to be cheerful and look for the good points in all situations.

5 *positive / brave*

I don't often try new things. Taking risks makes me nervous.

6 *outgoing / scared*

2 Now write the opposites of these adjectives. Use the words from Exercise 1.

1 brave ....
2 sensitive ....
3 shy ....
4 negative ....
5 adventurous ....
6 intolerant ....
7 selfish ....
8 inconsiderate ....

3 Circle the most appropriate adjectives for the people below. Then write another one.

1 movie stars and pop stars – *shy / outgoing* ....
2 mountain climbers and explorers – *adventurous / stupid* ....
3 doctors and nurses – *selfish / sensitive* ....
4 soldiers and police officers – *scared / brave* ....

Describing people

39 **4 Complete the dialogues using the words below. Then listen and check.**

adventurous negative outgoing positive scared responsible shy tolerant

1 **Michael** I don't think Miranda should be on the debate team. She's too [1]............................... to speak! We need people who are more [2]............................... , people who aren't afraid to be the center of attention.

Billie I think you need to learn to be more [3]............................... , Michael. Not everyone is the same as you are! Miranda will become more confident. Just give her time.

2 **Fatima** You're really going to rappel from the top of that bridge? What if you hurt yourself? I could never be as [4]............................... as that. I'm [5]............................... of going up to the top floor of our three-story building!

Oliver That's because you're so [6]............................... . You always think of the bad things that could happen. Look on the [7]............................... side for a change!

Fatima I don't agree. I don't always think of the bad things that could happen. I'm just [8]............................... , that's all. What you think is brave, I sometimes think is stupid!

Grammar

Reported speech

1 Complete the sentences with the simple past of *say* or *tell*.

1 He .... me to come inside.
2 Ivan .... that he couldn't come to the party.
3 We .... the teacher that we'd forgotten our homework.
4 Mary .... me she was going away.
5 The driver .... he would be late.
6 He .... us that there had been a terrible traffic jam.

2 Now write the direct speech for the reported sentences in Exercise 1.

1 ".."
2 ".."
3 ".."
4 ".."
5 ".."
6 ".."

3 Write the sentences in reported speech.

1 Jenny: I'm going to visit my relatives in Canada.
....

2 Patrick: I'm disappointed. I haven't been chosen for the team.
....

3 Luke: My mother won't be at home this afternoon.
....

4 The class: Mrs. Brown, we have a present for you.
....

5 Everyone: This is the best class we've ever had!
....

6 I: Penny, I'll call you later.
....

7 Mr. Todd: There's someone on the phone for you, Angela.
....

8 I: "Steve, I want to ask you a question."
....

Reported questions

4 **Write the original questions.**

1 He asked me what I was doing in his room.

....

2 He asked me where I had put his CD.

....

3 They wanted to know if they could buy tickets online.

....

4 They asked if there was anywhere to go for a pizza.

....

5 She asked me to help her with her science homework.

....

6 I asked Laura whether she was going to the club.

....

7 Helen asked Jon if he had enjoyed the movie.

....

8 Brian asked me to go out with him.

....

5 **Complete with *what, who, where, how, why,* or *when*.**

1 I asked Tim .... he was going. "Japan," he said.
2 I asked him .... he was going to get there. "By plane."
3 I asked him .... he was going with. "My parents."
4 I asked him .... they were going there. "My dad's working there."
5 I asked him .... they would be coming back. "In two weeks."
6 I asked him .... he was going to get me. "Wait and see!"

6 **Imagine you're a rock star. You just finished an interview. Use reported questions to write about the interview.**

1 He asked me ....
....
2 ....
....
3 ....
....
4 ....
....
5 ....
....
6 ....
....
7 ....
....

Grammar

7 Read the dialogue. Then complete the summary in reported speech.

Son I don't want to go to school today, Mom.
Mom Why not? Are you sick?
Son No, I'm not sick. But I hate school.
Mom Why do you hate it?
Son Because nobody likes me and everyone calls me names behind my back. They don't listen to me, and they laugh at everything I say.
Mom But you have to go to school, son.
Son Why, Mom?
Mom Because you're 53, and you're the principal!

Someone was lying in bed one morning. He didn't want to get up. He told [1]............................... to school that day. She asked if he [2]............................... . He replied that he [3]............................... but said that [4]............................... school. His mother [5]............................... it. The son answered that [6]............................... and everyone [7] .... back. He said [8]............................... and they [9]............................... His mother then told [10]............................... He asked [11]............................... he had to go to school. She said it was because [12]............................... the principal!

Skills

Reading

1 Read the article and choose the best title.

a) People who are bullied
b) Bullying—both sides of the story
c) I was a bully at school

Your turn to speak out

Rebecca used to be bullied at school. However, as she tells us now, she thinks people who are bullied should talk about their experience.

Rebecca says that many people who are bullied suffer in silence. She says that although she had always heard a lot about bullying, she didn't think it was going to happen to her.

Rebecca told us that the bullying started when she was in junior high school. People started calling her names and teasing her about being a good student.

She went on to say that every time she answered a question correctly in class, everyone would start jeering and saying that she was too smart for them.

She told us that by the end of the year she had become sick because she was so upset by the bullying. She began to hate school. But luckily she had friends who she could confide in, and they told the school counselor about her problem. She admits that talking to him helped a lot. Together, they talked about ways to deal with the problem, and the bullying stopped.

Rebecca's advice? Don't blame yourself. Nobody deserves to be bullied. But if you don't tell anyone what is going on, nobody will know that you need help.

Fourteen-year-old Dave used to be a bully. He admitted that he used to tease other kids and call them names. He said he used to bully the shy students, because he knew they wouldn't say anything. Dave said that although he could see that they were scared and upset, he couldn't stop. It gave him a sense of power. He then told us about the problems he had been having at home. He realizes that he was trying to get attention and help, but in a very negative way. But talking to a counselor helped him, too. "I hadn't thought about how much pain I was causing others," he said. "My counselor told me to put myself in their shoes, and it really worked. I just wanted to tell them all how sorry I was."

2 **Read the article again. Who said the following? Write *Rebecca* or *Dave* or *Both.***

1 there had been problems at home ....
2 name-calling had been part of the bullying ....
3 talking to someone had helped ....
4 trying to experience being bullied had helped ....
5 bullying had been a way of asking for help ....

Listening

40 **3** **Listen to an interview and answer the questions.**

Welcome to Teens Against Bullying!

Home
What we do
About me
How we can help
Email a question
Links

1 When did Hayley start the website? ....
2 What happened when she was bullied at her first school? ....
3 Who did she talk to at her next school? ....
4 What did she help to set up there? ....
5 How did they help students? ....
6 What happened after the presentation to the school council? ....
7 How can she help people through the website? ....

Writing for your Portfolio

4 **Your friend tells you he/she is being bullied by someone at school. Write a dialogue of about 10 lines between yourself and your friend. Ask your friend questions and give advice. Then write a short summary of your conversation using reported speech.**

UNIT 12 A fair world?

41 **1 Complete the dialogue using the phrases below. Then listen and check.**

it's not your fault	it wouldn't be so cheap	I'll remember
if it wasn't so cheap	they won't get jobs	you wouldn't buy it

Sasha Do you like this jacket?
Mick Yes, it's great. Is it expensive?
Sasha No, it's really cheap. Actually, 1 .... , I wouldn't be able to afford it.
Mick I'm sure 2 .... if you knew why it was so cheap.
Sasha What do you mean?
Mick Well, does this label say that it's a Fair Trade product, or does this store sell Fair Trade goods?
Sasha Oh, I think I know what you're trying to say. You mean, if the store didn't pay the workers who made this jacket so little, 3 ....
Mick That's exactly what I mean. Don't worry, 4 .... I watched a documentary about Fair Trade recently.
Sasha So why do the workers accept so little money for their work in the first place?
Mick I don't think they have much choice. If they demand more money, 5 .... So it's up to us to demand more money for them!
Sasha Well, if I buy anything, 6 .... what you've told me.

2 Match the sentence halves.

1 If you don't buy products with a Fair Trade mark
2 If you found out that your favorite clothes were made by children,
3 If people stop buying non-Fair Trade products,
4 If people didn't need money so badly,
5 If you were a farmer,
6 If we knew more about Fair Trade

a) workers around the world will benefit.
b) most of us would support it.
c) you can't be sure workers have been paid a fair salary.
d) wouldn't you want to be paid the right price for your products?
e) would you still wear them?
f) they wouldn't agree to some of the jobs they have to do.

Talking about what you would have done

3 Complete the answers to these questions.

What would you do if …

1 you bought something and two weeks later, it broke?
take / back / ask for / money back ....
2 you locked yourself out of the house and there was no one home?
climb over / neighbor's fence / ask for help ....
3 you walked into a party and then realized your shirt was inside out?
pretend it / a new fashion ....
4 you found a lot of money on the sidewalk outside a store, and after you picked it up you noticed a homeless person watching you?
give / half the money ....

Language Focus

Vocabulary Workplaces

1 Match the words and definitions.

1 factory	a) a place where a judge works
2 laboratory	b) a place where scientists experiment
3 prison	c) a place where a yoga instructor works
4 gym	d) a place where products are grown
5 mine	e) a place where goods are kept before they are sold to stores
6 farm	f) a place where criminals go after their trial
7 court	g) a place where products are made
8 warehouse	h) a place where minerals are dug out of the ground

Talking about places

2 Correct each sentence in two different ways.

Example: Miners work on a farm.
Miners work in a mine. / Farmers work on a farm.

1 A yoga instructor works in *an office*. ....
2 A *gym* is a place where criminals go. ....
3 *Judges* work in an laboratory. ....
4 People who dig things out of the ground are called *warehouse workers*. ....
....
5 A *scientist* works in a factory. ....
6 *Warehouse workers* work in a laboratory. ....
7 *Farmers* work in a warehouse. ....

42 **3 Complete the dialogues using the words below. Then listen and check.**

do scientist instructor where works work does

1 **A** What does your mother .... ?
B She [1].......... in a gym.
A What's that?
B It's a place [2].......... you go to exercise.
A Is she a receptionist?
B No, she's a yoga [3]..........

2 **A** What about your father? Where does he [4]..........
B He's a [5].......... , so he works in a laboratory.
A What's that?
B It's a place where he [6].......... experiments.

Grammar

If-clauses (review)

1 Complete the sentences with the correct form of the verbs in parentheses.

1 If you buy Fair Trade products, you .... farmers get a fair price for their goods. (help)
2 If I .... more time, I'd go check out that new designer store downtown. (have)
3 I .... that jacket if I had the money. (buy)
4 If I .... you, I wouldn't do that. (be)
5 How .... to school if buses aren't running tomorrow? (you get)
6 If labor .... so cheap in some countries, the things we buy would be more expensive. (not be)
7 Even if she .... me to her party, I wouldn't go. (invite)

2 Answer the questions about the sentences in Exercise 1.

1 Which are about possible situations in the future?
2 Which are about situations that we don't expect to happen?

3 Circle the correct option.

1 Would your parents be mad if you .... home late?
a) come b) came c) will come
2 I'd ask the teacher for help if I .... you.
a) will be b) am c) were
3 I'll tell him you called if I .... him later.
a) see b) will see c) saw
4 If we .... wasting energy, we'll destroy the environment.
a) won't stop b) don't stop c) didn't stop
5 Will the plane take off if there .... a storm?
a) be b) was c) is
6 If you .... a famous person to be for a day, who would it be?
a) chose b) could choose c) can choose

4 Write sentences using the second conditional.

1 If I have my own plane / I / go on a trip around the world.
....
2 If I have to move to another country / I / go to Australia.
....
3 If I get a car for my birthday / I / take you for a drive.
....
4 If I have a cat / I / call it Molly.
....
5 If I see someone cheating / I / tell the teacher.
....

5 **Complete the sentences with the correct conditional tense.**

If I [1]........................... (save) a lot of money this year, I [2]........................... (be able) to go on vacation in January. I like skiing so I want to go to Colorado. If I [3]........................... (book) the trip early enough, I [4]........................... (get) a discount on the price. If I [5]........................... (have) more money, I [6]........................... (be able) to go skiing every year!

6 **Write the questions. Use the correct conditional tense.**

Example:
Where / you / go / you / can choose / anywhere?
Where would you go if you could choose anywhere?

1 What / you / do / you / have / a day off school?

....

2 What / you / miss / you / live / in another country?

....

3 What / you / do / you / finish school early today?

....

4 How / you / celebrate / you / do well on your final exams?

....

7 **Now write answers for the questions above.**

1 ....
....

2 ....
....

3 ....
....

4 ....
....

Skills

Reading

1 **Read the article and then circle the correct answers.**

Cocoa farmer Kwame Agyeman and his family talk about the changes Fair Trade has made on lives in their community.

Kwame Agyeman

In this region of Ghana, we depend on the money we get from cocoa to buy everything we need: food, clothes, school fees, and medicine. But in the past, what we got paid was never reliable. Sometimes we didn't get paid at all. Now, the coffee company we work for pays all the farmers a fair price for their cocoa beans, and they pay on time and in cash. Even if the price of cocoa beans drops, we will still get a secure income.

Lindi Agyeman

If it wasn't for Fair Trade policies, I wouldn't be able to send my children to school. When my mother was sick, I had money to send her to the health clinic. Fair Trade has literally saved her life and has made life better for all of us. In our village, we have used the extra money that Fair Trade has brought us to build new wells for storing water. Without this, we would have continued to walk for miles every day to collect water from the river. The water was often dirty and made us sick. If we didn't have these wells, many lives would be lost from disease.

Koli Agyeman

I'm very happy that we have this well. This is the first time our village has had clean water. If we sold more of our cocoa beans to Fair Trade companies, we would be able to improve our village facilities even more.

1 How were workers paid in the past?
a) in cash b) irregularly c) fairly

2 How do workers prefer to be paid?
a) in cash b) by check c) by having schools and wells built

3 What happens to workers' income if the price of cocoa beans drops?
a) They don't get paid. b) They get paid the same. c) They lose their jobs.

4 What has the article taught you about schools and hospitals in Ghana?
a) They are far away. b) They are free. c) You have to pay for them.

5 How was Lindi able to help her mother when she got sick?
   a) Her mother was able to drink fresh water.
   b) She was able to pay for her to go to a health clinic.
   c) She was able to give her money.

6 What would happen if there wasn't fresh water in these villages?
   a) More people would die of diseases.
   b) Villagers would have to leave their homes.
   c) Villagers would have to buy water.

Listening

43 **2 Take the quiz. Then listen and check your answers.**

1 How many children around the world do not go to school?
10 million / 40 million / 80 million
2 How many adults in the world are unable to read or write?
29 million / 455 million / 771 million
3 If girls were educated like boys, how many lives would have been saved in the past year?
100,000 / a million / 100 million
4 If we want to provide education for all, how many more teachers will we need by 2015?
15,000 / 150,000 / 15 million

44 **3 Listen again and complete the summary.**

1........................... million children around the world are currently not in education, mostly 2........................... . There are at least 3........................... illiterate adults in the world. 4........................... percent are 5........................... . In some countries, such as Burkina Faso and Niger, only one in 6........................... girls goes to school.
If girls were educated like boys, 7........................... lives would have been saved in the past year. This is because educated 8........................... are in a better position to improve their own health and the health of their families.
There is a shortage of 9........................... teachers to provide a good education for boys and girls around the world.

Writing for your Portfolio

4 Read the situations below then choose one and write a short description.

- If I had my own car/house/job, I would ....
  ....
- If I work hard this year, I will ....
  ....

Grammar Review

Simple present — Unit 1

The *simple present* tense is used for habits and routines and to talk about facts.
I / You / We / They play football every Saturday.
The game starts at nine o'clock.
I don't eat meat.
My brother doesn't drive.

Present continuous — Unit 1

The *present continuous* tense is formed with the **simple present** form of **to be** + infinitive + **-ing**. The **-ing** form is the same for all persons, singular and plural.
I'm having lunch right now.
We're watching a DVD.
They aren't studying.
He isn't listening to music. He's talking on his phone.

The *present continuous* is used to talk about actions that are in progress at the time of speaking.

Present perfect — Unit 1

The *present perfect* tense is formed with the **present** tense of **have** + **past participle**:
They have finished their work.
I have seen the movie.

The past participle of regular verbs is formed like the *simple past*, by adding **-ed** to the infinitive of the verb.

The *present perfect* is used for past actions whose time is not specified.
Ben has left school. He's gone to China for a year.

The *present perfect* can be used with **ever** in an interrogative clause and with **never** in a negative clause:
***Have** you **ever skied**?*
*No, I've **never skied**.*

The *present perfect* can also express an action beginning in the past which is still continuing. It is often used with **for** (denoting a duration) or **since** (denoting the point in time when the action began):
*I've studied English **for** three years / **since** I was eleven.*

Past continuous
Unit 2

The *past continuous* tense is formed with the **past** tense of **to be** + infinitive + **-ing**:
What were you doing last night?
Paula was doing her homework, and I was playing a computer game.

The *past continuous* is often used with the *simple past*, to show that one action was in progress at a time in the past when another completed action (in the *simple past*) occurred.
I was having a shower when the phone rang.

It is also used with **while** or **as** to show that two actions in the past were happening at the same time.
While *I was waiting for the bus, I was listening to music on my MP3 player.*
I was thinking about summer vacation ***as*** *I was lying in bed.*

Past perfect
Unit 2

The *past perfect* tense is formed with the **past** tense of **have** + **past participle**:
He hadn't been at school for a few days, because he'd been sick.

The *past perfect* is used to show that one action in the past happened before another.
When I got to the concert, the band had started to play.
I had just finished my breakfast when I heard the doorbell ring.

Should / shouldn't and *ought / oughtn't*
Unit 3

Should and *shouldn't* are used to say what we think is a good idea, and to give advice. They are followed by the infinitive of the verb.
You should buy things online. It's so much easier.
You shouldn't tell anyone your bank account number.

We can also use *ought to* + the infinitive of the verb. We don't use *ought* as often as we use *should*.

Gerunds
Unit 3

A **gerund** is the **-ing** form of a verb. It can be used as the subject or as the object of a verb.
Shopping is my favorite hobby! (Subject)
I like ***swimming*** *and* ***playing*** *tennis.* (Object)

Talking about the future

Unit 4

Be going to / present continuous

We use **be going to** + infinitive to talk about future intentions.
I'm going to study drama when I'm in college.
What are you going to do when you arrive in Paris?
Shannon's going to design her own dress for the party.

The *present continuous* is also used to talk about the future. We usually use it to talk about fixed arrangements for the future.
I have a job in the summer. I'm working in a store.
We're having a barbeque on the beach on Saturday.

Future time clauses

Unit 4

As soon as, when, before, and *after* are often used to talk about actions in the future. In these phrases, the verb is in the present tense:
Please knock on the door before you come into the room.
I'll call you as soon as I get home.
When I graduate, I'm going to travel for a year.
Let's go get lunch after the class ends.

so / such

Unit 5

We can use *such* before a noun and *so* before an adjective to emphasize the quality of the noun or adjective. We can also talk about the result by adding *that* followed by a clause.
*It was **such** a nice day that we decided to have a picnic in the park.*
*I was **so** hot that I jumped right into the water.*
*I'd never been into **such** a wonderful building before.*
*I was **so** tired after our trip to the theme park.*

Phrasal verbs

Unit 5

Verbs followed by a preposition that cannot immediately be understood by looking at the individual words, are called *phrasal verbs*. The meaning of the verb often changes depending on the preposition following it:
take after = be similar to; **take up** = start a new hobby or activity; **turn into** = become;
turn off = use a switch to stop a radio or other device from operating
turn up = increase the volume;

The passive

Unit 6

The *simple present passive* has the following structure:
Subject + **simple present** of **be** (**not**) + **past participle**.

French is taught in most schools in Canada.

The *simple past passive* has the following structure:

Subject + **simple past** of **be** (**not**) + **past participle**.

The festival was held in June in Wisconsin.

make / let / be allowed to

Unit 6

Make + **object** + **infinitive** without "to" expresses obligation:
*She **made** the teacher really angry when she didn't listen.*
Let + **object** + **infinitive** without "to" is used to express permission to do a certain action:
My parents don't let me listen to music while I do my homework.

The passive form of *let* is the verb **to be** + **(past participle) allowed**. The past participle is the same for all persons, singular and plural.
Are you allowed to be out later than midnight?
Fran isn't allowed to wear makeup.
We aren't allowed to use cell phones in school.

will / won't

Unit 7

When we are sure about something in the future, we can use *will* (='ll) or *won't* (= will not) plus the infinitive of the verb.
There'll be food and drinks at the party.
I won't be late.
Will you come with me?

Question tags

Unit 7

Question tags are short phrases added to the end of a sentence to ask for agreement.
An affirmative sentence is followed by a negative *question tag*; a negative sentence is followed by a positive *question tag*.
He likes swimming, doesn't he?
You've met Tom before, haven't you?
They aren't American, are they?
She didn't go to the party, did she?

could, might, may for speculation

Unit 8

We can use *could, might,* and *may* to talk about possible situations and hypothesize about a situation. As always, these modal verbs are followed by the infinitive without *to.*
Jo may study physics next year.
The bus could arrive any time between 5:00 and 6:00.
I might go to the concert tonight, but I'm not sure.

-ed vs. *-ing* adjectives

Unit 8

Some adjectives have two forms: *bored/boring, confused/confusing, surprised/surprising,* etc. Generally we use the ***–ed*** adjective to describe the feeling we have.
I'm confused. (= I don't understand something.)

We use the ***–ing*** adjective to describe the thing that produces that feeling.
The work was confusing. (= It made me feel confused.)

used to

Unit 9

Used to (didn't use to) expresses a past routine:
We ***used to*** *go to the mall on Friday nights, but we don't any more.*
We ***didn't use to*** *have a dog, but now we have one.*

The interrogative form *did ... use to?* is rarely used.

Gerunds after prepositions

Unit 9

Many verbs and adjectives are followed by a *preposition.* If we want to use a verb after the preposition, the verb is in the ***-ing*** form.

Our teacher insists on speaking only English in class.
I'm not very good at running.
Is Jeremy interested in learning judo?

Present perfect continuous

Unit 10

The *present perfect continuous* tense is formed with the **person** + **have** + **been** + **ing** form of the verb:

Something smells good in the kitchen. Have you been baking?
Yes, I've been baking bread.

The *present perfect continuous* is used to show that something has been in progress for a certain period up to the moment of speaking and is still going on.

Embedded questions

Unit 10

Embedded questions are questions that are hidden in a sentence.
They often begin with *I don't know ......, Nobody knows ......, I have no idea. ......*, etc. The question word follows the expressions above:
When does he arrive? = I don't know ***when*** *he arrives.*
How do you find the answer? = Nobody knows ***how*** *to find the answer.*

Reported speech

Unit 11

Reported speech is a construction used to relate someone's opinion, message, or statement, without necessarily using the speaker's exact words. *Reported speech* is usually introduced by the verbs *say* and *tell. Say* can be followed by *that* but not by an object.
She ***says (that)*** *she wants a drink.*

Tell is usually followed by an object pronoun and can then be followed by *that.*
Sam ***tells me (that)*** *he is in drama club.*

When *reported speech* is introduced by *say* or *tell* in the *present* tense, there are no changes. The tenses are the same as in the direct speech:
"I am writing a test." He ***says (tells me)*** *that he's writing a test.*

If *reported speech* is introduced by *say* or *tell* in the *past*, tenses change as follows:
simple present ➔ simple past
"I am going home." She said that she was going home.
present continuous ➔ past continuous
"We're leaving in five minutes." They said that they were leaving in five minutes.
simple past ➔ past perfect
"You didn't do the work." The teacher said that I hadn't done the work.
present perfect ➔ past perfect
"I've been to the library already." She said she'd been to the library already.
will ➔ would
"I will see you tomorrow." He said that he would see me the next day.

Some subject pronouns in direct speech change as follows in reported speech:
I ➔ he / she
you ➔ I
you (plural) **➔ we**
we ➔ they

Reported questions

Unit 11

When we report a question, we use verbs such as *ask*, *wonder*, and *want to know*. Tense changes are the same as for reported speech (see page 79).
If the question has a question word such as *when/how/why*, we use the same question word in the reported question.
"When is Janet coming?" He ***asked*** *me when Janet was coming.*

If the question doesn't have a question word, we use the word *if* or *whether* in the reported question.
"Can I sit here?" I ***wondered*** *if I could sit there.*
"Will you help me?" She ***wanted to know*** *whether/if I would help her.*

If-clauses

Unit 12

Use the **first conditional** to talk about things that are possible or likely to happen in the future. The first conditional is formed with the *If*-clause: If + subject + simple present + main clause: subject + *will/won't* + infinitive.
If I get home early enough, I'll call you.

We use the **second conditional** to talk about situations that we don't expect to happen. The second conditional is formed with the *If*-clause: If + subject + simple past + main clause: subject + *would/wouldn't* + infinitive.
If I found a nice secondhand jacket, I'd buy it.

To ask a question using the first or second conditional, you simply reverse the word order.
Will you call me if you get home early enough?
Would you buy a secondhand jacket if you found a nice one?